LEADERS IN LIBRARIES

STYLES AND STRATEGIES
FOR SUCCESS

By
Brooke E. Sheldon

AMERICAN LIBRARY ASSOCIATION
Chicago and London 1991

Cover and text design by Charles Bozett

Composed by Charles Bozett in Galliard
using QuarkXPress 3.0

Printed on 50-pound Glatfelter,
a pH-neutral stock, and bound
in 10-point C1F Carolina cover stock
by Braun-Brumfield.

The paper used in this publication meets the minimum requirements of American
National Standard for Information Sciences—Permanence of Paper for Printed Library
Materials, ANSI Z39.48–1984. ∞

Library of Congress Cataloging-in-Publication Data

Sheldon, Brooke E.
    Leaders in libraries : styles and strategies for success / by
Brooke E. Sheldon.
        p. cm.
    Includes bibliographical references.
    ISBN 0-8389-0563-3
    1. Library administrators. 2. Library administration. 3. Leadership.
I. Title.
Z682.4.A34S49 1991
025.1--dc20   91-8678
                                                       CIP

Printed in the United States of America.

95 94 93 92   5 4 3

Dedicated to:

Ann Barnett,
Administrative Assistant, School of Library and
Information Studies, The Texas Woman's University,
whose approach to her job, her family, and the
community demonstrates a perfect blending of
management skills and leadership qualities.

CONTENTS

ACKNOWLEDGMENTS

Warmest thanks to the many colleagues who gave time and energy (mostly between conference sessions) to be interviewed. They provided a wealth of material, of which only a fraction is contained in this book. Some are quoted extensively, others barely mentioned, but each provided important insights that made it not only possible, but imperative, to share them with others.

Special appreciation to faculty and students, past and present, of the School of Library and Information Studies at Texas Woman's University. It has been a wonderful and indulgent environment in which to test ideas and practice differing management and leadership styles. Thanks, too, to Warren Bennis for providing that initial encouragement.

Specifically, the following persons have not only enriched the content of this manuscript, but also provided stimulus, incentive, and encouragement:

Adeline, Agnes, Al, Allie Beth, Ana, Ann, Anne, Arthur, Augusta, Barbara, Bernie, Betty, Beverly, Bill, Blanche, Bob, Bridget, Carlton, Charles, Charlie, Charlotte, Chris, David, Dee Dee, Dennis, Dick, Don, Dorothy, Duane, Dwayne, Ed, E. J., Elaine, Eleanor, Elizabeth, Elliott, Elsie, Eric, Eugene, Evan, Evelyn, Fanny, Felipe, Foster, Frank, Fred, Gail, Gary, George, Gilda, Gracie, Harold, Harriet, Hazel, Helen, Herb, Herman, Jan, Jay,

Jean, Jerrold, Jesse, Joe, Joel, John, Joyce, Julie, June, Keith, Ken, Larry, Lee, Leigh, Leonard, Lester, Linda, Lona, Lotsee, Lottie, Lowell, Mae, Maggie, Margaret, Marie, Mary, Mary Alice, Mary Ann, Mary Jo, Matthew, Maxine, Miriam, Nancy, Nettie, Norman, Page, Pamela, Pat, Paul, Paula, Pauline, Peggy, Penny, Phyllis, Prentice, Ralph, Richard, Rita, Robert, Roger, Russ, Sam, Sara, Sarah Rebecca, Scott, Sharon, Shirley, Steve, Susan, Tom, Toni, Warren, and Willard.

INTRODUCTION

I've read a lot of leadership books and they're all right and they're all wrong . . . it depends on a match between the style and circumstances and individual personalities.

Richard Dougherty, Professor
University of Michigan

Many decades have passed since my mother sent me off to college with a trunkful of new clothes and a handful of proverbs, like "Be all you can be" and "To thine own self be true." At the time, of course, I paid little attention to these homilies, but in the past few years, while experiencing the challenges of teaching public library administration and the basic management classes to graduate students at Texas Woman's University, those time-worn phrases have become more meaningful. To teach library management is to become fascinated with the attempt to integrate procedural skills with the behavioral elements that are critical for success in any organization.

Along with millions of others, I have assiduously devoured many of the management texts and best-sellers of the late seventies and early eighties, searching for those elusive essential factors that lead to administrative excellence. From Drucker to Waterman, I read them all, and as each new theory comes along, my long-suffering students examine it, discuss it, compare it with other current fads, and finally accept or reject its validity for the organizational climate of libraries.

1

It was in this context, in early 1987 at a San Francisco airport, that I happened to pick up a copy of the best-selling *Leaders: The Strategies for Taking Charge* by Warren Bennis and Bert Nanus. The authors had interviewed ninety leaders—sixty CEOs, all corporate presidents or chairpersons of boards, and thirty from the public sector. From these interviews, the authors developed four strategies or "kernels of truth" that they felt characterized all ninety of the leaders.

As I read through *Leaders*, it appeared to be a useful book for class discussion—as a text, or at least for supplementary outside reading. The problem, however, was that while concepts were universal and somewhat generalizable, the examples used were of corporate leaders. Surely there were leaders in our own profession who would be more valid role models for both practitioners and students of library management.

By the time the plane touched down in Dallas, I had finished the book and made a decision. I would replicate Bennis' study, that is, ask exactly the same questions, but ask them of library leaders. The purpose of the study would be to gain an understanding of the qualities held in common by leaders in the library profession. Having isolated these characteristics, I would then compare them to those of corporate leaders as identified by Bennis and Nanus. The general hypothesis would be that the differences, if any, between corporate and library leaders are insignificant.

In my initial enthusiasm for this idea, I reasoned that not only would the study provide interesting data to improve and authenticate my management classes, but it might also be of interest to relatively new librarians, and even those in mid-career who wished to improve their leadership skills. Bennis believes that leadership is "the marshaling of skills possessed by a majority but used by a minority. But it's something that can be learned by anyone, taught to everyone, denied to no one." He goes on to say that "only a few will lead nations, but more will lead companies. Many more will lead departments or small groups. Those who aren't department heads will be supervisors, and so on."

That plane trip initiated a most wonderful journey for me. The opportunity to talk at length with sixty distinguished members of the library profession has been deeply rewarding. Not one person turned down the request for an interview, although several persons were missed because of geographical or time constraints. In any case, I have included mention of the styles and strategies of a number of other librarians who, while not specifically interviewed for this study, exhibit many of the qualities identified by Bennis.

To those who will immediately ask what the conceptual basis for the study was, how the sample was derived, and other valid questions concerning methodology, it can be said that in structuring the interviews I asked exactly the three questions Bennis asked: What are your strengths and weaknesses? Was there any particular experience or event in your life that influenced your management philosophy or style? What were the major decision points in your career, and how do you feel about your choices now? To those questions I added two: What, if any, has been the influence of mentors on your career? How do you feel about the future of the profession?

There are, of course, serious limitations to this kind of research, the most obvious being that it is based on the assumption that the persons identified as "leaders" have the ability to accurately evaluate their strengths and weaknesses. Also, this research is not measuring behavior as perceived by others; in fact, many studies using the model of a leader's self-perception have been shown to be statistically unrelated to descriptions of the leader by others.

On the other hand, observation of the leader by others presents many difficulties as well. It is more than the possible bias of the observer and the inability to control variables. In any case, even situational approaches to studying leadership assume that while the style of leadership likely to be effective will vary according to the situation, some leadership styles will be effective regardless of the situation. But it seemed important to start somewhere, and because very little has been done in our field on leadership, it seemed that a replication of Bennis' study would be a good place to begin.

The leaders interviewed met one or more (usually more) of the following criteria: director of a major public or academic library, nationally recognized school librarian, executive director of one of the major library organizations (SLA, ALA, ARL, etc.), dean of a library school (selected by peers), or state librarian. Several other persons who control major resources, or by reason of their position or professional activities have a powerful impact on the profession, were also interviewed. Like Bennis and Nanus' selection, the selection of these individuals was intended to be somewhat representative, but by no means inclusive. Sixty other library "leaders" would have done just as well.

What were the qualities that Bennis identified? Basically, there were four "kernels of truth," or strategies, or human-handling skills, that the leaders possessed. These were:

1. attention through vision
2. meaning through communication
3. trust through positioning
4. positive self-regard

Certainly Bennis' ninety leaders had many other qualities that aided in their success, but these four—intensity (usually concerning the mission of the organization) that induces others to join in; outstanding communication (and listening) skills; ability to be consistent and thus develop trust; and self-confidence—were the four distinguishing traits that emerged over and over again.

As one reads Bennis' book, there is much overlap among these qualities. For example, the quality of possessing vision overlaps with meaning through communication, and so on. That is, it is essential to have vision, but meaningless if one is unable to communicate it to others. In attempting to categorize the responses from the library leaders, I too found tremendous overlap and infinite redundancy. But after I sifted endlessly through the interview transcripts, central themes began to emerge, and the chapters that follow describe how the library leaders said they manage their organizations.

There are many similarities between this model and the model of Bennis and Nanus, and some differences. There is also evidence that in tune with current management trends, our leaders have been among the first to shift away from a somewhat mechanical model of planning and efficiency focused primarily on assessing needs, setting goals and objectives, and so on. The new approaches do not throw out the systematic approach, but they place much more emphasis on creativity, risk-taking, innovation, and even intuition. Our library leaders find enormous satisfaction in their work, and this satisfaction appears to equate with success. The entire topic is enormous; this book is not an attempt to cover it all, but simply to provide some insights from those who shape our professional image. The chapters that follow attempt to identify those qualities and strategies that bring both satisfaction and success.

Chapters 1 through 4 discuss the four characteristics as isolated by Bennis. Chapter 5 discusses the role of mentors in the development of library leaders. Finally, chapter 6 provides recommendations for leadership education in librarianship.

1

VISIONARY LIBRARIANS:
Achieving Results by Securing
Commitment

We have the least demanding, most uncritical mass of con-
sumers . . . in an information-based world they are grateful for
every crumb, so if we know what should be done, and what is best
to do, and if we don't stand up for and fight for the very best . . .
then we default, and we let the profession down.

Carlton Rochell
Dean of Libraries
New York University

Bennis and Nanus say that "management of attention through
vision is the creating of focus," and they declare that every single
person they interviewed had an agenda. Normally, we think of
an agenda as a fairly straightforward set of goals to be accomplished with objectives, time lines, and so forth. The leaders undoubtedly have detailed plans, but they also have an extraordinary capacity to separate their vision from the planning assigned
to others. This gives them enormous flexibility about detail,
while still maintaining close communication with colleagues and
subordinates. Bennis claims that "leaders are the most results-
oriented individuals in the world" and that every single one of
the ninety people they talked with were not only results-oriented, but also often "like a child, completely absorbed with creating a sand castle in a sandbox, they draw others in" (p. 28).

The library leaders possess this quality to an enormous degree, although curiously enough, not many of them describe
themselves exactly this way. Rather, they often talk about their

ability to get others involved and to energize people so that projects are accomplished. In fact, they have their dreams, their visions of what will be accomplished, and many have demonstrated that they have the personal drive and magnetism to capture attention, draw people in, and move forward with them toward a common goal.

One of the more clear-cut instances of this ability is the story of the emergence of the national library symbol. Elizabeth Stone, who is now Dean Emerita of the School of Library and Information Science at Catholic University, set her mind and heart on the adoption of a symbol when she was President of the American Library Association (although she was not the first person to suggest the idea). When she first broached the idea in 1981 during her inaugural address in San Francisco, it is safe to say that most of those assembled saw little hope of its being accomplished. By 1985, however, the symbol not only gained the approval of the ALA Council and the Federal Highway Commission, but could (and can) be seen on many highways in many states and in hundreds of communities, large and small, from Alaska to Florida. The blue-and-white sign has here, in Canada, and elsewhere become almost as familiar as McDonald's golden arches. As one of Stone's associates said, "She has the tenacious spirit to not only articulate a goal, but to bring people together, write the letters, make the phone calls, and [like a child absorbed in a sand castle] simply persist until the job gets done." Literally hundreds of ALA members and other librarians worked to make the library symbol a reality, but what put it all into motion was the absolute conviction of Stone that it should and could be done.*

Creation of a library symbol was a national effort, largely a volunteer effort, and there are other examples of effective results-oriented organizational leadership that came to light in the interviews, but incidents are drawn mostly from the professional positions held by those interviewed.

At this point, it should again be emphasized that none of

---

*The library symbol was designed by Ralph Devore for Western Maryland Public Libraries, and Bob Garen of the Detroit Public Library chaired the ALA Committee on Library Symbol Implementation. It was accepted by the Federal Highway Administration for inclusion in their *Manual on Uniform Traffic Control Devices* in 1985.

the interviewees was asked specifically whether he or she had a "vision for the library" or clear-cut goals. Rather, interviewees were simply asked to describe their strengths. For many, the importance of a clear and well-articulated agenda was paramount.

Bob Warner, now Dean at the University of Michigan's School of Information and Library Studies, says that when he became Director of the Michigan Historical Institute, it was terribly ill-housed and not very well known.

> I had three goals I set for myself: I wanted to give it a national reputation, I wanted to raise its visibility, and I wanted to give it an adequate home—that meant a new building because it would never be able to flourish in the existing circumstances. This was very difficult because there were no state appropriations, no thought of that, so what you had to do was bring together a whole group of people, very diverse elements, to work toward a common goal. . . . we developed a friends organization, and we garnered support from many sectors . . . and both political persuasions, including a Republican congressman and a Democratic governor . . . to get people like that to subsume their differences to see that this is an important objective, and to come out and give a lot of money for this, was a big challenge, and we did do that. Then, of course, the same thing was tested when we tried to get the [National] Archives independent— we'd been trying for twenty-five years to do that, and to be sure there are a lot of reasons . . . (this is a complicated story, which I want to write some day) . . . but, the fact is that you had to bring people together. . . . the biggest chore, it seemed to me, was an organizational one. Again, all the components it takes to get legislation focusing and moving in concert in a systematic way toward achieving that goal. I think I put the pieces together. I didn't do it, no one person could do this sort of thing, this group did it, that group did it, the other group did it. But, if they were all isolated actions, it would never have happened. How it all came about is a very intriguing story, but we managed it, did the impos-

sible and did get the law passed creating the only independent agency in the Reagan administration when everyone said, "This will never happen; we've been trying
thirty years and it's not going to happen," particularly in
this hostile administration. But, it did happen . . . and
that was probably the most important, without doubt,
the independence of the National Archives is the most
important thing I will have accomplished in my life; there
is no doubt. That is it. You don't do those things very often.

Warner now sees himself in the third phase of his career,
charting the future course of education in librarianship and information at the University of Michigan.

Jim Haas, President of the Council of Library Resources,
characterizes the process as one of "setting your sight on what
would be the best possible thing, not under the naive assumption you'll ever get there, but to make certain that if you do
certain things, you go in that direction rather than in some
other direction." He goes on to say that the "obligation is not
to run the library efficiently . . . [the] obligation is to ensure
equitable access to information."

Kathleen Heim, now Dean of the Graduate School at
Louisiana State University, has a remarkably similar view.

Have a very clear sense of what you want to accomplish,
and always have it so big that you can never accomplish
it. . . . I always keep in mind why I'm doing something
and try to make a clear goal and that's to get information to people better. And I try now to only do things
that fit in with that, and to turn down things that don't.

In discussing his years as an academic library administrator
and as a dean, Ed Holley, now Kenan Professor at the University of North Carolina–Chapel Hill, notes how important it is
to be a student of the organization, "able to articulate goals."

I always felt there were two or three major things you
want to accomplish. If you got other things accomplished, that was wonderful, but you better be sure of

what your priorities are, that everybody understands what those priorities are, and that you are able to articulate that to all the constituencies you are dealing with . . . and those same people who think they are great communicators, and they understand where they believe they are leading their organizations—but the people who are trying to do what the leader wants done, either don't understand it or are frustrated because they feel that they don't know what the two or three major things are. Whitman says "to have great wits you must have great audiences." You have to encourage those people to fit their personal goals and objectives, professional goals, with the organizational. And that's hard.

Bob Hayes, former Dean at UCLA, when asked about his strengths, talked first about the respect he has for the people he deals with, the faculty and students. "I have avoided diminishing the role of anybody. I listen to what they say and try to represent what they say, but *I have my own agenda, and I pretty much follow it.*"

Successful library leaders are indeed results-oriented, and they can and do inspire others, but it seems apparent that there is a difference—an advantage, if you will—that librarians and not-for-profit professionals have over many of Bennis' corporate leaders. Corporate leaders can and do find that their work is meaningful, satisfying, and even important for humankind, but the bottom line in the corporate world is outcome, and outcome translates into profits. Our library leaders have a deep and intense belief that what they are doing is not only satisfying, but deeply significant.

"The thing I love about librarianship is its infinite possibilities," says Penny Abell, University Librarian at Yale.

My two most important strengths are that I know what an academic library is there for; that I have a very clear sense of the scholar and student in my head all the time, and I help my colleagues in the organization to understand that what they want and need isn't the important thing. Now that sounds trivial, but I think it's not, and I think it's the most important concern whether we are talking public libraries or school libraries or whatever. It's to have a very clear sense and close identification with the clientele . . . and I love universities, and I love scholars, and I love their idiosyncrasies; and they're important people to me and to our enterprise.

I am very skilled at identifying and attracting first-rate people into the organization. I'm probably good at it because I learned early on that there's just no way you can have (and by the way, wherever I am is going to be the best library of its kind that exists) . . . you cannot have the best library without the best people, and that takes a lot of work. I just put an awful lot of my effort into recruitment and development . . . and I search the country. We search the country to tell everybody they can to look everywhere they can to find the brightest, most able people who are most suited to that particular situation, and we interview up, down, and backwards.

And then I think in the course of those interviews I'm able to articulate . . . this sense of aspiration for excellence that we have and the particular strategy or priorities that we have at a given time. And people find that attractive . . . and they find the people they meet elsewhere in the organization attractive, and we try to give everybody a very broad exposure. Again, not original, but effective.

This deep commitment to the importance of the job and the worth of the profession is very often the first idea expressed when these librarians begin to talk about their strengths, the whys of their success. As one listens, it is obvious that while every individual has an intense satisfaction in his work, this has to be transmitted not only to staffs, but also to colleagues and other constituencies.

Bill Summers, ALA President in 1988–89 and Dean at Florida State's School of Library and Information Studies, says, "I've never regretted one day going into this business. I have never had a day in which I did not feel that I took out of it a great deal more than I put into it."

In a lighter vein, but with equal intensity, Lee Brawner, Executive Director of Oklahoma City's Metropolitan Library System, describes his job in this way:

> I enjoy the hell out of what I do. I really enjoy it. I frequently on weekends may be out playing tennis with some other guys, and they will begin moaning about the "Monday syndrome," and they look upon me as a weirdo because I'm excited to be getting back to the work at the library and the opportunities at hand. That has rarely waned.

"A noble profession," says Patrick O'Brien, Director of the Dallas Public Library. This sentiment is echoed by Pat Woodrum, Director of the Tulsa City-County Library System, who literally radiates satisfaction in her job and excitement about the future of libraries.

At least one of the leaders not only expresses a passion for librarianship, but also worries about lack of commitment on the part of others. Gary Strong, State Librarian of California, says:

> I believe firmly that a lot of library leadership and library managers have forgotten what the profession is all about—they might as well be managing widgets rather than managing an institution that's very, very special; it's not a widget shop. I've tried to structure organizations that believed in the user first. And then the bureaucracy. I mean you've got to get things done, that's reality. But I think you can do it humanely, and in a caring fashion. I really get irritated with those in our profession who do not have the "passion of the profession." I look for passionate librarians. They give a damn about what we are for—librarians not ready to give in to the pressures of charging fees and selling out the public trust, as I call it.

It seems that the leaders' tremendous confidence in the value of what they do is a powerful force in enabling them to achieve their goals. Bennis and Nanus do not identify this phenomenon, but it seems to work in the following way for the library leaders. They are able to be quite flexible in the methods they use to accomplish a goal because the ultimate worth of the goal warms and sustains them.

Nettie Taylor, retired State Librarian from Maryland, talks about this in relation to State Library development.

> I'm comfortable with ambiguity, and I expect that is a weakness, but I have tended to think that people who have a really specific hard-bound plan and don't know how to modify it as time goes on . . . the results don't turn out as well in the end.

Taylor also stresses the dependence any good administrator (and particularly one in state library development) has to have on others to accomplish goals.

> Anything that happens happens because the people out in the state want it to happen. . . . if you can't get one library system to move and do anything, you know you have a dozen or two dozen others to work with. . . . Go over there and feel good about working with somebody who really wants to do something.

Patrick O'Brien puts it another way:

> There is almost never going to be any perfection in public agencies, and people do come up with different ways to do things. If the end result is the same and it doesn't do any harm, you must let people feel they have accomplished something. If someone comes up with an idea, and you say, "Here's a better way to do it," it's not likely to get done. That's really important.

With few exceptions, the interviewees found themselves echoing Russell Shank, Director of Libraries at UCLA, who says, "I'd rather see what should be done than to do it," or Dick DeGennero, Librarian at Harvard College, who says:

[I am] impatient with a lot of detail, and I address the big picture, but there is a lot of stuff that I'm sometimes willing to jump over because it's too detailed and it's boring and it's hard work . . . analytical work that needs to be done before you set sail on one of these binges. So the best thing I can do is try to get some people around me who will keep me honest and who will ask those difficult questions, and do some of that analytical work, check out the ideas and directions.

Toni Bearman, Dean of the University of Pittsburgh's School of Library and Information Science, says, "While I am persistent in reaching a goal, I am not one who should be in charge of implementing a project. I would not be a good associate director of a library who has to see that everything happened, and happened correctly."

In similar vein, Agnes Griffin, Director of the Montgomery County Libraries in Maryland, acknowledges, "I don't like to finish things. I like to start them. . . . I'm much better at breaking ground and then leaving, and this is the first time that I have stayed longer than six years in one job, so I am having to live with my mistakes."

Another characteristic that Bennis finds and that the library leaders have in endless abundance, is persistence. Warner notes:

While sometimes I'm not tough enough, on the virtuous side, I am tenacious and persistent. I wear people down, not by shouting at them, but by pleasantly reminding them of the situation until they can hardly stand it and they finally give in to it to make me go away. Creative bugging, I call it. I still use it. Don't shout at them, find different ways and different guises to bring up the same issue over and over again.

Sometimes for the librarian it is the gift of enabling others to understand vividly what is meaningful about what we do—to be able to express ourselves in terms that the average person, whether on the staff or in the external community, understands. While we think of communication as a different aspect of leadership (and we will discuss it in depth in the next chapter), this ability to conceptualize is central to a leader's ability to command the attention needed to realize the vision.

Bob Rohlf, Director of the Hennepin County (Minnesota) Library System, tells a story of going to a budget hearing for the county board of commissioners.

> We were probably the most heavily used public institution that they dealt with, and I could just see that they didn't believe me one bit . . . and I said, "I'd like to explain that to you by saying that last year more people used your public libraries than went to see the Minnesota Twins, the Minnesota Vikings, the Minnesota North Stars, and the Minnesota Strikers combined; and we [the library] didn't get three pages of news in the paper every day. But we impacted more people than all of those teams put together." The commissioners understood exactly what I meant because they had been in those stadiums, and they could see all those people. You must present information on the layman's terms. If I went to the commission and said, "We are one of the few libraries in the U.S. serving over a half million people, with a circulation of twelve per capita," there would just be blank looks. It doesn't mean anything.

Just as Reagan captured the attention of the American people when he compared the national debt to the height of the Empire State Building, librarians must be able to evoke sharp imagery. Bob Rohlf gives another example.

> Last year I went into a budget meeting, and I brought in a whole bunch of books, and I piled up two stacks of books, and I had another item in a sack, and they didn't know what it was. I said, "This number of books is what the average citizen in the county took out of our libraries last year, and this is the number they used in the library." I reached in the bag, and I brought out half a book, and I said, "This is the number of books we bought last year. Now you've got to do something

about that." An administrator came up to me afterwards and said, "That was the most effective audiovisual presentation I've ever seen." And I said, "Why? It's just a fact."

It could be argued that this ability to conceptualize an idea for staff or the public is not a "visionary" skill, but rather a communication skill, and indeed there is a great deal of overlap. One is most certainly useless without the other. What comes through in talking with the library leaders is that this ability to conceptualize is very closely tied to a quality that many of them describe as an essential attribute for success—an ability to "see the big picture." They see themselves, as do Bennis' leaders, "concerned with their organizations' basic purposes and general direction." Their perspective is "vision-oriented." They do not spend their time on the "how to's," the proverbial "nuts and bolts," but rather with the paradigms of action, with "doing the right thing."

Bob Wedgeworth, Dean of Columbia University's library school, says, "I tend to concentrate on big things, and I let a lot of problems solve themselves." On the other hand, Joe Shubert, the New York State Librarian, who is known throughout librarianship not only for his leadership, but for his meticulous attention to detail, acknowledges that too much attention to the "nuts and bolts" may be a weakness. He also argues that because he "pays attention," he is "better able to see that bigger picture, and a lot of people complain that they have difficulty seeing the bigger picture."

Richard Werking, Director of Libraries at Trinity University in San Antonio, says, "I'm interested in administering and managing . . . not many directors are." He also credits his success in getting good things accomplished in the library to a president who is "unusually detail-oriented and on top of what's going on."

Tom Galvin, former Executive Director of ALA and now Director of an interdisciplinary doctoral program in information science at the Rockefeller College of Public Affairs and Policy in Albany, expresses it this way: "I'm hell on detail. I can get through enormous amounts of work and grasp and retain the smallest details. This, of course, can be very useful . . . but can also be a weakness. Any strength carried to an extreme becomes a weakness."

Norman Horrocks, Vice President of Scarecrow Press, is known throughout the profession for his scrupulous attention to detail. For many years, in various posts, he has kept the ALA Council (and the Board), as well as several other organizations, constitutionally correct. For many people, this would be the most tedious of tasks, but Horrocks does it with such dispatch and humor that his frequent forays to the microphone are welcomed by his colleagues.

Ann Prentice, formerly the Director of the library school at Tennessee, now the Vice President for Information at the University of South Florida, says, "I'm good at seeing the whole picture, conceptualizing, prioritizing," and quotes a colleague who described her as "visionary, but not off the wall." Aware that she tends, like many Yankees, to be low-keyed and not show how she feels, she says, "I may not come on strong, but I wear well . . . and I have trained myself to pay attention to the details . . . work through the bureaucratic details with my students."

Joe Shubert talks about the realities of leadership at the state library level, the difficulty of becoming fixated on the achievement of a single goal without "neglecting other things." He also articulates the difficulty inherent in the work of public agencies like state libraries. Shubert says there are few problems that libraries can solve or that they should try to solve by themselves, yet many planners have that kind of mentality. "If it's literacy, for instance, they don't like it because the people in elementary and secondary education capture all the literacy monies . . . but the only way that you can create change, solve problems, is through those kinds of boundaries. Libraries should be content to just have a piece of it, but people don't like to work in that way. They have an institutional view rather than a global view."

The skillful leader has the ability to recognize this need for ownership. Because Shubert understands this phenomenon, he is extremely patient in working with diverse groups and constituencies. He understands that this patience and cooperation pay off because he is trusted, and he is trusted because he understands that not only the labor, but the rewards, must be shared.

This ability to form coalitions to achieve our visions and goals is important in contemporary society and is particularly important in libraries, where as often as not, the library is an information or a facilities resource. It is not always the catalyst in initiating new ventures. Library leaders are also players; they move easily from one role to another.

Shubert also exhibits that quality described by Bennis as characteristic of the new leaders. He pays attention to the tasks his staff is involved in and thereby creates a "sweeping back and forth of energy" that enables the organization to move forward. Kathleen Heim describes it as

> trying to identify people who are going to be good. . . .
> I can identify the ones that are going to be leaders
> themselves. I get them involved in projects, their energy
> feeds off mine, mine off theirs, and we get a lot more
> done than anyone can expect.

There is no doubt that a leader's understanding and interest in routine tasks can be inspiring. The key is to achieve the right balance, interest, knowledge, and even excitement about details of the plan, but encouraging, not forcing, staff members to make decisions about how a project will be carried out.

Bennis and Nanus say that their leaders told them over and over again that

> they did the same things when they took charge of their
> organizations—they paid attention to what was going
> on, they determined what part of the events at hand
> would be important for the future of the organization,
> they set a new direction, and they concentrated the attention of everyone in the organization on it. We soon
> determined that this was a universal principle of leadership [p.88].

If leaders also are players in devising plans, staffs become deeply involved in shaping the plans because they feel they are part of a team. Perhaps this is why Liz Stroup, Director of the Seattle Public Library, describes herself as a coach. She says, "Client-centered service is my passion. . . . I want every client treated as if she were my mother. . . . I want every member of our staff to be empowered to break any rule if it makes sense."

When members of an organization share the vision of its leader, they are empowered because they understand that they are part of something important and that their work will make a difference. In such organizations, decision making is widely diffused throughout the staff because they understand what the end results should be.

REFERENCE

Bennis, Warren and Bert Nanus. *Leaders: The Strategies for Taking Charge.* New York: Harper, 1985.

2

COMMUNICATION:
How Library Leaders Use It to
Achieve Organizational Goals

W hen the Chancellor calls you up and says, "I've got tickets to
the basketball game, would you like to go?" you go. First of all,
you're glad he called.

Beverly Lynch, Dean
Graduate School of Library
and Information Science, UCLA

Chapter 1 touched on using metaphor to conceptualize for others the importance of an idea. Leaders must not only have this
ability, but also find other ways to communicate their vision and
goals so that all members of the organization can understand
and internalize them. Leaders must also find a high degree of
satisfaction in helping these persons achieve the goals.

In *Leaders,* Bennis and Nanus discuss how this understanding, participation, and "ownership" of the vision is created.
Bennis says the mechanism that must be used is the "social architecture" of the organization, "which can facilitate or subvert
the best-laid plans" (p.111).

Social architecture as defined by Bennis has to do with "a
shared interpretation of organizational events so that members
know how they are expected to behave . . . also generates a
commitment to the primary organizational values and philosophy . . . serves as a control mechanism, sanctioning or proscrib-
ing particular kinds of behavior" (p.112). What does Bennis
mean by "shared interpretation of organizational events"? Let
us suppose that the organizational event is the emergence of an

irate patron. Almost every librarian would agree with Liz Stroup that the client comes first, but there is in many libraries a wide variation in how this value is operationalized. The more disagreement there is among staff, the lower the level of consensus about the meaning of "client-centered service," and the lower the degree of commitment.

Intensity of expression ("client-centered service is my passion") is a powerful way to shape the social architecture; follow-up to allow staff to reshape old rules to implement this value is even more powerful. Note that the idea is to allow staff to reshape the social architecture in the sense that how the new rules and regulations should be reshaped is not prescribed. Our library leaders communicate a "bottom-up architecture." A leader's communication style can encourage a process of interpreting democratically organizational events because style can carry values of respect, trust, and caring.

Our library leaders communicate in many different styles, but the basic formula for success seems to belong to the person who: (1) places emphasis on values simply stated and develops one or two understandable themes—themes that then become the dominant message of the organization, (2) has a talent for listening, and (3) has an understanding that the value of power is in sharing it.

When David Henington, Director of the Houston Public Library since 1967, was asked to name his strengths, he said:

> I am a people person—I like to go in and get it functioning, gain the confidence of people, get people working together on a common goal. What works is to define a problem at the simplest, most elemental level. If you play the role of expert, it is harder to communicate what you are trying to do . . . especially with City Council and groups. . . . we must talk on a level that people understand. Sometimes the staff thinks I'm oversimplifying things . . . but I listen, and I learn, and I restate in basic terms . . . and it works for me.

Because ours is a relatively technical field, there is often a temptation to provide too much detail—almost a compulsive need to show that we understand the complexities of the problem and to bring staff or outside groups up to snuff on an issue. The reasoning here is that if they understand it all, they will accept the idea. The truth is, people are much more captured by clear and simple ideas. When too much information is presented, the group gets bogged down in details. The leader's job is to talk about *what* should be done. When there is consensus and commitment, the details of *how* will fall into place.

Our leaders are skilled in following this basic and simple process: First, a message is conveyed. It inspires responses. The leader listens to the responses and synthesizes them, interacting with staff, task forces, groups, and others. The leader then repeats the message—it has not lost its intensity, but it has captured the concerns *and the commitment* of the staff. At this point, it becomes relatively easy for the leader to delegate the details of implementation.

Some of our library leaders speak eloquently about the art of listening and its central importance in their work. Tom Phelps, Head of Library Programs for the National Endowment for the Humanities, talks about

> the frustration in the listening. Did you hear it right? Did you hear enough of it? Listening and then trying in a skillful way to put those ideas together in a coherent whole; getting support for those ideas (not just financial) and then giving it back. Those are the things I'd like to think I do . . . and in some regard, I think I have been successful in not having to internalize it and be in control of everything, letting it go at the time it needs to be let go . . . watching and leading again, but then moving on to other things, and then you just start the cycle over again: listen, then create, then support, and then give it up.

Phelps' position is not unlike that of those leaders who staff our library associations, who are often marvelously creative (such as ALA staffers Peggy Barber, Roger Parent, and Margaret Myers), but whose jobs exist essentially to provide the means for others to look good. Library association directors have more visibility and recognition, but walk an even more tenuous line between exercising leadership and mirroring the concerns of an ever changing corps of volunteer and elected officers.

Association staff members, as a general rule, are experts in the art of listening, and it is perhaps this quality, more than any other, that makes for success in association management. Management texts tell us that about 80 percent of work time is spent talking with others. The higher one's job level, the higher the percentage of time spent communicating. It is, therefore, extremely significant that so many leaders stress the importance of listening skills.

As John Gardner noted in *Leadership Papers*, a message on the computer terminal is not enough, nor is a suggestion box. "Nothing can substitute for a live leader [not necessarily the top leader] listening attentively and responding informally. . . . wise leaders are continuously finding ways to say to their constituents, 'I hear you'" (pp.23–24).

Perhaps the person in the library profession who has had most influence on our listening skills is Professor Sara Fine of the University of Pittsburgh. Fine, a psychologist who teaches in the library school and has conducted workshops on interpersonal skills in many states and internationally, says:

> Leadership is not a comfortable role, particularly if one assumes that it means one must be liked by everyone, one must know everything, one must control all activities. Perhaps the only measure of successful leadership is the realization by the group that the leadership function has been transferred to the group itself, and that it is the group that has responsibility for its own direction and its own success [Penland and Fine, p. 18].

Even those few library leaders who say that they are not particularly good listeners recognize this as a weakness and try to compensate for it. E. J. Josey, Professor at the University of Pittsburgh and past President of ALA, admits:

> I can't always listen and see the other side when I become

so passionate about my own concerns. . . . sometimes I have to literally force myself to step back to listen to what the other fellow is saying and sometimes there is merit in another viewpoint, but I find this process very difficult.

Elliot Shelkrot, Director of the Free Library of Philadelphia, ranks his enthusiasm for the job and his strong listening and interpersonal skills as key factors in gaining commitment from staff. He says, "Vulnerability is the key to good communication." Shelkrot, who was an enormously successful State Librarian of Pennsylvania, (he worked against many obstacles for a number of years to achieve a statewide library card, and now "Access Pennsylvania," like Connecticut's card, is a model for other states), in discussing his weaknesses, notes that he has always had a "certain lack of self-confidence—particularly when starting a new job." This admission, which is rare among the leaders, seems to reinforce his statement about vulnerability. He is not afraid to admit that he sometimes lacks self-confidence. This quality pays off for him in interpersonal relationships. People like him for his vulnerability, which they recognize as being genuine, and therefore they want to help him. This goes against the popular belief that leaders should always appear brave, strong, and invincible. Granted, we don't want them to be wimps, but it is extremely important for leaders to share their fears, along with their dreams of the future. Generally, this is done most effectively on a one-to-one basis or in small groups, but a really eloquent speaker can do it with a cast of thousands.

If our leaders were polled on this issue specifically, undoubtedly most would say that the ability to listen and interact well is of far more importance than the ability to make speeches, yet several of the leaders have said that they wished they were more articulate and could think faster on their feet. Dick DeGennero speaks of avoiding situations early in his career where he would need to speak to large groups, and he regrets that now.

I'm probably better at communicating in writing [and] that's my technique for developing my vision for the organization. It's during the process of trying to write out a five-year plan, or to write an article on a subject . . . it's that process that causes me to know, after I've written it, what it is that I believe. Sometimes I start to write one thing, and I end up coming out on the opposite side. But in the technique of verbally influencing people and communicating that vision, I do better in small groups and one-on-one conversations and in small group meetings.

While DeGennero's superb writing skills more than compensate for possible podium inadequacies, there is no doubt that strong public speaking skills are generally viewed as a decided asset by the library leaders. Several of them mention this quality when enumerating their strengths. "I'm great at giving a speech, out in public," says Linda Crismond, ALA Executive Director. Bill Summers also cites this talent. "I don't know where I got this attribute, but I think very well on my feet . . . and so I tend to be at my best at things like budget hearings and presenting proposals where people are asking you questions."

Joe Rosenthal, Librarian at University of California–Berkeley, who has a reputation for being one of the best listeners in the field and who is a highly creative administrator, says, "I'm not an inspiring public speaker—it's difficult for me to seize the moment and make witty remarks. . . . I do envy people who can say just the right thing."

One of the most articulate of our leaders, Eric Moon, former President of Scarecrow Press, confides, "I'm terribly nervous about speaking always . . . and I don't like doing it, but you have to overcome that fear." Moon reminisces about the Library Association when he was extremely active, speaking all over England:

I couldn't get over this nervousness, and they had a speaker there who was one of the senior ministers in the government who was the most fluid, articulate speaker I had ever heard in my life, hardly used a note, so cool. And I went up to him afterwards and said, "God, that was incredible. Would you tell me how you can do that sort of stuff without being nervous?" And he said, "My boy, if ever you get up there and you are not nervous, you won't be worth a damn." So that encouraged me a bit.

Moon also describes chairing a meeting in New York when John Lindsay then Mayor of the city, was the speaker.

> I was sitting next to him when he was at the lectern, and his hands were visibly shaking. . . . they said the same thing about Kennedy at his inauguration, his hands were shaking at the podium. The only thing you learn through experience is how to hide it completely so that people won't know . . . and I think I've learned to do that.

Two of the best "off-the-cuff" speakers (both for content and articulation) in the profession are Arthur Curley (Director of the Boston Public Library) and Grace Slocum (retired Director of the Cecil County [Maryland] Public Library). Both Curley and Slocum have wonderfully resonant voices, and both were members of the ALA Board. When they approached the microphone in an ALA Council meeting, they easily commanded the full attention of a sometimes distracted Council. Overall, although many wish they were more articulate, our library leaders are accomplished speakers and (at least outwardly) comfortable at the podium.

In discussing their strengths, the leaders make it clear that while listening and being able to communicate on multilevels are extremely important skills, a major strategy most of them try to use is one of empowering staff, enabling them to do the things they want to do.

Bob Rohlf talks about his ability to share power with his staff.

> My idea is to give the staff as much chance to make a mistake as possible because they're going to learn from it, which is the way I learned . . . to support them in decision making right up to the point where I think there's any kind of a dangerous political problem, and then I'll take the responsibility and make the decision.

As an example of how he shares decision making, Rohlf describes the hiring of personnel.

> I totally changed the hiring practices to a point where the supervisors appoint their own staff totally, right up the ladder. I only appoint four people in the whole library system; those are the four that report to me. Sometimes I've never even met the new people. The supervisors come in and tell me who they want to appoint and why, and they know I have the veto power, and I've exercised it once in sixteen years, and that was an internal promotion. (When I shared information I had with this relatively new supervisor who wanted to make the promotion, she agreed and appointed her next choice . . . but otherwise that's all.) In my organization, I'm legally responsible for appointing everybody, but I don't even sign the forms anymore. I think that's a reflection of my style in that I hold the person responsible for what he or she does; therefore, that person should be responsible for who he or she appoints. I should not appoint people.

Rohlf was asked how he applies this decision making to long-range planning. That is, in setting goals for the organization, to what degree do directives come from the top?

> The goal, the purpose of it, comes from the top, but the details come from the staff. I just appointed another automation task force to produce the next stage plan for whatever automation efforts we need and said that at the end of its investigation and study period we expect a recommendation on whether we should or should not adopt the new catalog, what kind of catalog it should be, whether it should be integrated or whether it should be a dual system, what it should include. The task force knows the money is technically available. Go out and do your recommendations. And I will not serve on the task force. That's about as open as I can get.

Rohlf, along with many other library leaders, is especially proud of his attempts to get people to not only grow in their own jobs, but also to take a broader view of things and eventually move on to bigger responsibilities.

Getting staff to take that broader view is mostly a function of showing that they are trusted and also a matter of coaching. A strong administrator does not believe for a moment that a talented staff member will stay with her indefinitely. Rather, she takes an active role in helping that staff member outgrow his current position.

Rosabeth Moss Kantor has coined the term *segmentalism* for a style that "divides the organization into tiny territories and then tells all to stay within these confines" (p.204). Successful library leaders tend to be extremely accessible to their staffs; they spend time visiting in different departments. It is not a chore for them to spend time listening to individual staff members because they are intensely interested in everything that goes on. They insist that departments talk with each other and that there is wide and open sharing of information. At the same time, they adhere to Bennis' premise of simple values and simple themes.

The excitement library leaders exude about this profession, their global view of its potential, is contagious, but something more is needed. They must understand the staff, their hopes and plans for the future. Motivation for the staff does not miraculously occur; leaders need to uncover existing motives. As Bob Wedgeworth puts it:

> I think I'm pretty good at finding out what other people want and developing ways to achieve what I think needs to be accomplished in ways that allow them to do what they want. I think that the major part of leadership has to do with how you motivate people to achieve common ends. . . . Many people come to work, and I don't hold it against them, [but] their priority is their family . . . they look forward to vacations . . . they have hobbies, etc. . . . so I have always tried to pay attention to people and their interests. . . . I recognize, for exam-

ple, when they want flexibility with their vacation time or when they want time off to participate in church activities or are active in local political circles. . . . I try to make the job flexible enough to allow these things . . . and I find that when people can get what they want, they are a lot easier to work with, and it is a lot easier to achieve overall goals. . . . the way I use systems is to reduce variations in performance. I want people to perform at least at a given level, but above that level you have to motivate the individuals themselves. . . . the system won't do it.

Frank Lee notes in his dissertation on the contributions of Lillian Bradshaw, formerly Director of the Dallas Public Library:

Although accounts of leaders like Bradshaw tend to focus on bricks and mortar, this is not the dominating force behind her interest in public libraries. Certainly it is the most tangible dimension of the growth and development of the Dallas Public Library as a system—the creation of a strong branch system and the building of a 650,000-square-foot library. And certainly it may be her most tangible contribution to the City of Dallas. But it was not her focus. . . . Bradshaw's activities have always [reflected] her key ideas, values, and beliefs . . . virtually every speech, publication or conversation begins and ends with the *constituency* [emphasis added] of the public library. . . . her focus on the individual has remained constant throughout her career, at the heart of her philosophy of service [p.25].

Bradshaw not only worried about individual patrons; she was extremely involved in all of the social and political concerns of the people of Dallas as they struggled to shape Dallas into a progressive, culturally rich environment.

As one observes leaders in the library profession, it appears that those who are and have been the most effective communicators are those who stick to simple basic values and themes, reiterate them over and over again, and work closely with staff in making sure they understand what the basic message is and that it is shared by all.

Sometimes the message has as much or more to do with the process of giving service than the actual product. Pat Woodrum, in discussing her staff, said "We're a group that supports each other in what we do. . . . [We] kind of have a philosophy also that we're going to be very positive in everything that we do . . . it's contagious. If you go to work in the morning and people start smiling at you, you are forced to change your attitude." When asked how she has managed to instill this upbeat attitude, Woodrum said, "We've talked about it, and one of the things I've said is 'We are going to be glad to come to work on Monday morning'. . . . people begin to pick it up, and I'm very fortunate in having people around me that tend to be that way anyway."

An effective leader who wishes to change the social architecture of an organization must articulate the new values—over and over and over again— and the point that Bennis makes is that this transformation must begin at the top. It does not much matter the style of social architecture—formalistic, collegial, or personalistic;* what does matter is that the leader is easily understood and (as we will see in Chapter 3) totally consistent.

REFERENCES

Bennis, Warren and Bert Nanus. *Leaders: The Strategies for Taking Charge.* New York: Harper, 1985.

Gardner, John. "The Heart of the Matter." *Leadership Papers.* Washington, D.C.: Independent Sector, 1986.

Kantor, Rosabeth Moss. "Encouraging Innovation and Entrepreneurs in Bureaucratic Companies." In *Handbook of Creative and Innovative Managers,* ed. Robert L. Kuhn. New York: McGraw-Hill, 1988.

Lee, Frank. "Lillian Moore Bradshaw and the Dallas Public Library" (in "The Innocent Voyage to the Razor's Edge," unpublished diss., Texas Woman's University, 1988.

Penland, Patrick R., and Sara F. Fine. *Group Dynamics and Individual Development.* New York: Marcel Dekker, 1974.

---

*In *Leaders,* Bennis and Nanus describe three styles of social architecture: (1) formalistic, characterized by hierarchy, structured relationships, and decision by compliance, (2) collegial, characterized by peer relationships and consensus decision making, and (3) personalistic, which is individually oriented and characterized by actions aligned with self-concept (pp. 118–138).

3

TRUST THROUGH
POSITIONING

You start looking at what you learn when you don't succeed
and you begin building on that, and you do it as quickly as possible. Like the rodeo rider thrown off the bronc, you get right back
on because the longer you wait, the tougher it is to get back in
that saddle, so after a couple of breast-beating months, I formed a
new task force. . . . we put together a new campaign strategy, got
back on a ballot, and we won the election by an 89 percent margin . . . and it was very gratifying, to say the least.

Lee Brawner, Executive Director
Metropolitan Library System
Oklahoma City

Bennis says, "We trust people who are predictable, whose
positions are known and who keep at it; leaders who are trusted
make themselves known, make their positions clear" (p. 44). In
the last chapter, we talked about the absolute need for the
leader to get the message across and win acceptance for it, at
every level of the organization.

What Bennis finds in talking with corporate leaders is that
not only are they able to articulate a clear vision for their organizations, they are successful because they know how to position themselves and their organizations to achieve their goals.
The single attribute that helps the leaders achieve this is their
ability to maintain consistency between word and deed. They
say what they want to accomplish, and they do what they say.
Because they are predictable in this sense, the corporate leaders

have the ability to inspire trust, and thus acceptance, for their ideas, from staff, and also acceptance for their organizations externally.

During talks with library leaders, the quality that most of them project is one that is essential in inspiring trust—the ability to be consistent. Charles Robinson, the Director of the Baltimore County Library, talks about it in the context of organizational stability. Noting that he has been Director since 1963 and his assistant, Jean Barrie Moltz, came in 1964, Robinson says there has been very little turnover in top administration.

> So there's a lot of continuity here, and there's a lot to be said for the staff being able to count on you. You do what they expect, really, in a way, and so I figure that my successor, whoever she is, is going to have a tough time; and then her successor will be fine, once they get rid of the Robinson/Moltz aura around here.

Longevity in one position is one kind of consistency, and it is legitimate, but it seems more likely that, while Robinson is considered a risk taker, his staff can usually predict his reaction or behavior in a variety of circumstances. That is, they know what he will probably accept, reject, or consider further. They also know he will make decisions that are consistent with his belief that the public library must never become an elitist institution. This does not mean that he does not frequently surprise, and even shock, people. Robinson is iconoclastic and can be blunt, a quality that is often little appreciated, but few would argue against the premise that he is not only one of the most creative minds in the profession, but he also has had a tremendous influence on the development of public library service.

Interestingly enough, Robinson does not see himself as creative, and practically the first thing he said (when asked) in the interview was, "My greatest strength is hiring the right people to work with and letting them do the job, and another strength is *stealing other people's ideas* [emphasis added]. . . . people often have a good idea and then don't carry it out. . . . I never had a new idea in my life." He then goes on to say,

"Much of what I have become infamous for is ideas that have come from folks like Elliot Shelkrot and Tom Walker [now retired from the Maryland State Library], who dreamed up centralized selection."

Robinson is consistent also in that on most issues he takes a position that is in direct contrast to the accepted theory. He says, "I just get impatient with the conventional wisdom. I figure that if it's convention, it's probably wrong." One would think that this philosophy would drive staff crazy, but in reality, Robinson's somewhat unconventional style seems to work well because he is *consistently* unconventional, *predictably* unconventional, and those who work with him adjust to that style, and therefore it works.

If asked, most people would probably say that qualities they like in a boss include listening skills, thoughtfulness, and responsiveness, but in fact they often adjust to a person who describes himself as Robinson does: "I'm somewhat impatient, and I'm not particularly thoughtful, kind, or considerate in my treatment of people; I terrorize a lot of people." As one staff member said, "All that's true, but he really has a heart of gold."

The library profession is filled with leaders who are, in the best sense of the word, predictable. They let people know where they stand. Both in their jobs and in our national associations, there are thousands of examples. E. J. Josey is one. Josey has consistently championed the cause of human rights, both in his local community and in the American Library Association. Another example is the late Sam Whitten, Professor at the University of Texas–Austin. As Lee Brawner said in discussing this mentor:

> Sam Whitten taught me that in terms of espousing ideas and philosophies . . . you don't espouse them, you live them. . . . if you believe in intellectual freedom, then you defend it, at home and away. And he did it, and he never flinched in the face of challenges to that philosophy.

Ed Holley also talks about the importance of consistency:

Nobody has ever changed his or her style by reading a book. . . . if you are authoritarian, you're going to be authoritarian, and if you are democratic or participative or consultative, whatever you want to call it, you're likely to be that. . . . the likelihood is that the individual is not going to make many changes . . . and I think there are times when a firm hand is needed, and that means an administrator who likes to do things his or her way. . . . so long as it's consistent, and everybody knows that, then it's okay. . . . [Peter] Drucker says somewhere that the worst thing you can do is say you are one style and be another.

When Beverly Lynch, Dean of the Graduate School of Library and Information Science at UCLA, was asked if she uses any of the current management techniques, she said, "I don't believe in them." Lynch, who writes extensively on the theory and practice of management, believes that "organizations change all the time, and therefore what may have worked very well five years ago, won't now. . . . the trouble for a manager is knowing that change has happened and that the old ways don't work anymore." Lynch says, "My big worry is that you won't have anybody around you that will tell you you're all wet until there is some crisis. . . . most people just won't give you the bad news."

She does not say so, but based on her record, it appears that Lynch places a high value on the ability to speak up and say what is on one's mind, ignoring political expediency. In a public forum, Lynch brings the bad news as well as the good, unearths the problems before presenting solutions, and this approach has captured the respect of the library profession. Lynch worries about change, but her overriding characteristic is that she says what she will do and she does what she says. She has views. Without a viewpoint, one cannot be consistent, and if the leader has a strong point of view, she will be anticipatory rather than reactive.

Lynch touches on a topic that Bennis sees as essential to effectively "positioning" an organization. Establishing trust for

oneself is a very short step from establishing confidence in the
organization. Bennis says we do it by "creating a niche in a
complex changing environment." Seldom is this accomplished
by assuming a reactive stance; rather, it requires an aggressive,
proactive look at the needs of clients and potential clients and
the ability to develop new and better services to meet those
needs.

If this is true for the corporate environment, it is doubly important for libraries whose staffs must ceaselessly ask themselves: What business are we in? What values are more important than others? Bennis argues for proactive organizations, and
our library leaders agree, but they are also aware of the importance of knowing when to assume a slightly reactive stance in
order to keep options open in the light of changing circumstances.

The popular notion that the new executive must move
quickly to establish a power base is not shared by all of our library leaders. Dick DeGennero says:

> In a new position, I like to spend a lot of time learning
> the environment and learning who the people are and
> what the problems are. . . . I think it's a big mistake to
> make any important decisions before doing this. I know
> there are others who come into a situation like this and
> want to make their weight felt and make their presence
> felt, and who are quite willing to make decisions—even
> if some are mistakes, at least people will know that there
> is someone new in charge. That's not my technique.

Bob Wedgeworth reinforces DeGennero's comments.

> One of my fundamental management maxims is that
> early decisions, even if they are only half right, are better
> than delayed decisions, but I don't apologize for delay-
> ing because when I don't feel confident about a solu-
> tion, and can't really identify the reason, I tend not to
> act until I feel confident. Once I am clear about the cir-
> cumstances that I want to address, then it is very easy for
> me to move quickly.

Wedgeworth tells the story of General George Thomas, a cautious and deliberate general who ended up having the most significant victory of the Civil War—the Battle of Nashville.

> He was the only Union general to completely demolish a Southern army, and I always remember him for that reason. I put a lot of emphasis on early preparation and planning before you put something in motion. Anything of any complexity, I think you need to put the time up front and do that initial thinking and planning; be sure you have complete understanding of the problem before you move ahead.

On the other hand, Russell Shank says, "I worry a lot, think a lot, stare out the window a lot, but I also know if you over-think it, if you try to know everything before you take the first step, you're doomed to stand on one leg forever." Shank goes on to say that there is a learning period and techniques for learning about a new environment, most relatively simple. He likes to physically move around the library, asking a lot of questions,

> not trying to learn everything about what a person is doing, or what a department is, but question [and comments] like "Why is that over there?" "Well, explain that to me," "What are you doing?" or "Do you find that this is kind of stultifying, sitting all day at this machine?" You get engaged in conversations with people, and before long there's a mosaic of little pieces and parts that get put together in your mind . . . not asking the global questions, but the bits and pieces to put together a picture of the place. This works for me because I don't have to learn about the overall environment itself; I mean, the University of Wisconsin and the University of California at Berkeley and Washington and Columbia and UCLA are all universities, and roughly speaking, the same kind. They teach different things; they may teach different ways, might have different laboratories, but I know what the business is. You don't have to ex-

plain that to me. I know what a president or chancellor wants. . . . I don't conduct this bits and pieces inquiry as a conscious thing. I just like roaming around and talking to people. I've never really stopped to figure out if I'm offending anyone by being there or not. I don't feel any different inside me as the University Librarian at UCLA than I did when I was back in college washing out the garbage cans at the women's dorms at the University of Washington.

This "just likes to talk to people" style of Shank helps him put together the information he needs for decision making. It is not a style that everyone is comfortable with. Shank acknowledges that, for many people, an attempt by the University Librarian to sit down and engage in small talk with people on the job would simply make the staff nervous. But it is important to find creative ways to be in close touch with how the organization operates and who the key players are before any move is made to reposition the organization.

In the business world, it is known as understanding the corporate culture; in libraries, our leaders are sensitive to the traditions and norms (service ethics) of the organizations they lead. The editor of *Library Journal*, a publication that seeks to provide insight and perspective for the profession, John Berry talks about the importance of a "strong ideological commitment—a point of view that undergirds your work."

Evan Farber, Librarian at Earlham College, interviewed for *Libraries in the Nineties: What the Leaders Expect*, says, "In a college situation it means understanding the politics of the situation, the purpose of the personnel of the institution, to know it well, to know its history" (p.116). In fact, it goes far beyond mere sensitivity to and knowledge of the institution; for the most part, our leaders build trust not in the first one hundred days but cumulatively in the long term by personifying the values they attempt to institutionalize.

Our library leaders exhibit enormous patience when attempting to change the organization because they understand that staff cannot be coerced into accepting a new idea. It takes many attempts, endless meetings, before any change is accepted. More importantly, our leaders understand that no matter how creative or innovative the idea, how "right" it is for the organization, resistance is always present. As Bennis notes in *Leaders*:

> If everyone embraced the innovation, it would be difficult to take it seriously—as an innovation. Innovation causes resistance to stiffen, defenses to set in, oppositions to form. And any new idea looks either foolish or impractical or unfeasible at first. It takes repeated attempts, endless demonstrations, monotonous rehearsals before innovation can be accepted and internalized by any organization [p. 52].

Herbert White, Dean at Indiana University's library school, makes an important distinction between leadership and management in this regard.

> Many managers *seek* consensus, which is a determination of what the group wants, and what the group wants is assumed to be good even though history tells us that consensus is usually safe and free of innovative ideas. . . . Leaders, by contrast, do not *seek* consensus. They *build* it by persuading others to share their goals and their dreams [p. 5].

White sees leaders as those who seek conflict rather than avoid it, and rather than being "good soldiers who see that the objectives are achieved even if they disagree with them [role of managers] . . . leaders concentrate on ensuring that their objectives become the organizations' objectives." Sometimes this takes infinite patience on the part of the leaders.

Library leaders who were interviewed generally have tremendous confidence that their goals are right for their organizations, and they have clearly in mind their role in the achievement of those goals. As Russell Shank puts it, "There's a difference to me . . . I mean the person who manages . . . seeing that things get done, like automating the library. I don't know how to do that. . . . I'm a person who's an administrator or a leader. I know *what* to do; I don't know *how* to do it."

Shank's statement provokes two questions that are critical to any discussion of leadership in the library profession. The first: Is there a tendency for librarians (by natural disposition) to personify the *how*, the "do things right," mentality (manager) versus the *what*, "do right things," mentality (leader). The second question must be uppermost in the minds of those who hope to be leaders: How do I achieve the self-confidence of a Shank or a Sloan (Dean of Libraries, Columbia University) or a Shubert, and how do I know that what I want for the organization is the right thing?

Dick DeGennero has a somewhat reassuring response.

It's a question of age and experience. Young people, as they enter the profession, are so concerned about doing things right that they don't pay attention. . . . it takes age, experience and self-confidence to come to the conclusion that maybe what we are doing is not the right thing and there is need to change. . . . Some people are born with that; some of us have to work at it and develop it.

In the following chapter, discussion centers on how library leaders develop confidence or positive self-regard, and on the contagious effect this quality has on the organization.

REFERENCES

Bennis, Warren and Bert Nanus. *Leaders: The Strategies for Taking Charge.* New York: Harper, 1985.
Riggs, Donald E., and Gordon A. Sabine. *Libraries in the Eighties: What the Leaders Expect.* Phoenix: Oryx Pr., 1988.
White, Herbert. Unpublished *Library Journal* article, 1988.

4
SELF-CONFIDENCE:
Building Strengths and Compensating for Weaknesses

My father was a city fireman in a small city in Ohio; I was the first child [in the family] to go away to college. I, of course, went to college, therefore, thinking I was the most brilliant person in Western civilization. When I got to Harvard, I discovered that not only was I not the smartest person in Western civilization, I wasn't even the smartest person in my dorm room. I was number three of those three guys.

Bob Berring, Law Librarian
University of California–Berkeley

Just as the leaders in Bennis' study exude positive self-regard, our library leaders know that they are highly successful at what they do. When asked, they are never hesitant to discuss their strengths; but what *is* significant for the majority is that the first strength they mention has to do with human skills, the ability to work well with others to mobilize people to accomplish goals.

As Bob Hayes puts it:

One of my strengths is [that] I have respect for the people I deal with—the faculty and the students. . . . A second strength is that I am very open and honest with persons in the administration and faculty, and the outside world. . . . the result of that is an administration that believes what I tell them. They have no reason to doubt it.

Past President of ALA and currently Director of the graduate library school at the University of Washington, Margaret Chisholm says:

> As I try to analyze what seems to me to be things that I do with maybe greater strength than others, first of all, I think I'm very perceptive. I can pick up on nuances in body language, nuances in tones of voice. . . . I think that I can anticipate quite well what people are going to expect, demand, what their positions will be. . . . it's very accurate and intuitive. If I would compare the way I do things with the way I see others operate, I would say that's a skill I have in excess of the norm.

Noting that a major strength is her self-confidence, Chisholm explains that she grew up in a very small town, and by the time she was in the seventh grade, she was competing against seniors in high school.

> I was in all the plays . . . a cheerleader . . . editor of the paper . . . I was in the band . . . and I suppose that the circumstances may have contributed to a sense of self-confidence that might or might not have been justified. . . . it never occurred to me that there was anything I might not be able to do very well.

Elaine Sloan, Dean of Libraries at Columbia University, talks about how quickly strengths carried to extremes turn into weaknesses, but she sees her greatest strength as being "a real ability to empathize and connect with people . . . and some good interpersonal skills." But, says Sloan, "the flip side of that is that it is sometimes difficult [for me] to confront a 'personnel' problem, and the closer I am to the problem, the harder it is."

Robert Croneberger, Director of the Carnegie Library of Pittsburgh, says, "I love turning people on," and this "translates into skills in joint decision making and problem solving." Peggy Sullivan, Dean of Professional Studies at Northern Illinois University and former ALA President, describes herself as a "populist. . . . the ability to find out what the people want, to listen, and make decisions based on this is important for an administrator." Sullivan refers not so much to relationships with colleagues as to the importance of being totally in tune with the needs of the community, the clientele.

The library leaders' self-confidence comes through immediately. However, this respect for their own talents does not manifest itself in an egotistical way. Rather, the leaders are almost modest; it's as if, in their answers, they are trying to clarify as much for themselves as for the interviewer what works for them. Some, like Margaret Chisholm, attribute their self-confidence and success in part to childhood experiences. Others have a quiet, innate sense of self-worth. Elaine Sloan discusses her meteoric career:

> Someone on the search committee [at Indiana University] said, "You know, you came in and you were just so confident." And it never occurred to me until he said that, but it is true, I am. I tend to be confident in myself and my ability, but I thought that I could do that job, and that it was right for me. And as it turned out, it was.

When Patrick O'Brien was asked to describe his strengths, he said:

> I've always had a hard time determining just what I do that works. When I make mistakes, I know that I've made them, but most of the time, things that I've done have worked. My ability to get along with people has been the knack that has enabled me to work with even people that I don't like because the key in organizations is people. . . . it's the people who provide the services who make or break the organization. When you're in public service, your effectiveness depends on how you deal on a one-to-one basis with people. The way the organization is run has to have that strength about it also. I've seen organizations where the people skills were not

really strong, and consequently the way services were provided and attitudes of staff were all reflected in that, and service wasn't good.

Along with Margaret Chisholm, Patrick O'Brien goes back to his youth for an explanation of how he gained self-confidence and other qualities that work for him. O'Brien says it was difficult for him because, as a boy, he was

very shy, not outgoing. . . . I forced myself to talk to people, to get out of them what they want . . . and in doing that, I built my communication skills and ability to work with people. In every organization, there are frustrated people because no one will listen to them. If you keep that in mind, keep saying [to yourself] "listen, listen, listen"—and respond positively at least a third of the time, then you are probably ten times better than most administrators. Most people don't listen. They only hear what they want to hear—partial hearing skills—and it's reflected in how they respond. I think that is one of my strengths.

O'Brien goes on to say:

Any person who deludes himself into thinking that when you're on top you run the organization, it's not reality. Especially in large public libraries—there are so many interests. With twenty branches, you have twenty people who have been given an entire facility. We trust them to manage a fifteen or twenty thousand [square] foot building, the people in it, the mechanics of it, the services it provides. That's a big responsibility. . . . when you give people responsibility for an entire facility, you have to give them the authority—you're saying, "I expect you to run this branch—let me know if you need any help." I use "we" a lot more than I use "I." I still have a hard time thinking of myself as leader of a large organization—how I got here—why I got here. It wasn't something I had a great vision about; I liked what I was doing in public libraries, and the more responsibility the better.

Most of the interviewees stressed the importance of dealing-with-people skills. "Ability to work with people to accomplish a goal" (Jane Robbins, Director of the library school at the University of Wisconsin–Madison); "bringing diverse groups together to carry out a common theme" (Bob Warner); "I'm not a confrontationist. . . . I am someone who is able to listen and, I hope, judge fairly" (Robert Stueart, Dean of Simmons College library school); "communications—consensus building" (Ken Dowlin, Director of the San Francisco Public Library); "Well, I think I like people; I have a genuine appreciation for them. And when I say that, I mean all kinds, classes, sizes, creeds, cultures, and persuasions" (Jean Curtis, Director of the Detroit Public Library).

Not all of the leaders, however, select human skills and the ability to achieve consensus, as their major strengths. On the contrary, for a few people, these attributes wind up on the weakness side of the ledger. Eric Moon says:

> I suppose if I had to name one [strength], it would be lack of fear. I have a tendency, perhaps too much of a tendency, to say what I believe, whatever the consequences, to do whatever I believe, whatever the consequences. And that has brought me a lot of friends over the years, and it's also brought me a lot of enemies, but I don't believe you can get change, real change, accomplished unless you are prepared to do that. I used to talk to students about that all the time, and Larry Powell [Professor Emeritus, University of Arizona] has said the same thing—that if you're afraid, if you're not willing to put your neck on the line, you are not really going to have much impact on anything. And I at least like to think that for myself . . . that's true; it may not be, but that's at least how I'd like to be perceived.

Moon describes his weakness as "intolerance for stupidity, laziness, ineffectiveness" and his management style as a combination of autocracy and belief that everybody can do better than he or she is now doing. And what I used to do in most of the positions where I was a manager was first learn every job in the operation and then prove to the staff member that I could do it better than he or she could, so that if I needed to criticize that person, he or she knew it wasn't coming from ignorance. But those who have worked with me will also tell you that I have a very free-wheeling style; I'm inclined to let them go as far as the horse will take them, and I will support them against attack from anybody else whatsoever—not necessarily against attack from me, but from everyone else for sure.

Herbert White, lists his number one strength as energy. "I do not postpone," says White, "and I have the courage and willingness to tackle the problems." He sees himself as able to differentiate between idealism and the pragmatic, and "tries not to spend time on the undoable." While he candidly admits he is extremely impatient with bureaucracy and is more than willing to fight policy decisions, he has "no hidden agendas" and does not "hold grudges."

Lotsee Patterson, Coordinator of School Libraries in Oklahoma City and one of four Native Americans who holds a Ph. D. in Library Science, sees her greatest strength as "persistence . . . dedication . . . really believing in libraries . . . never giving up, and . . . always having a vision for the future . . . the place of libraries and how they will serve people, particularly Native Americans."

Our library leaders also talk candidly about their weaknesses—"too impatient," "do not suffer fools gladly"—but it is noticeable that they do not dwell on them. As in the case of Patrick O'Brien, some have systematically set out to compensate for them. Most do it by surrounding themselves with staff who have the qualities they see themselves as lacking. Except for the Galvins, Shuberts, and Kimmels and their ilk, most of our leaders are supremely happy to leave the details to others. When Richard Dougherty, Professor at the University of Michigan and ALA President, 1990–91, was asked about attention to detail, he said:

> I used to be a systems person and had a lot of ability in that area. . . . it was a strength. . . . it's not anymore because I'm involved in so many issues. Now I have a database that we maintain, projects I'm involved with—that at any given time may have from thirty to eighty items in it—so that there isn't a lot of time to devote to a single issue, only if it becomes a crisis or only if I become very interested in deciding it. But I delegate very well. Delegation is easy, and to me one of the biggest mistakes we make is to bring in strong people and fail to delegate. They make you look good—in fact, you may get people that are better than you are—and my job is to orchestrate it.

Not many of the leaders describe themselves as charismatic, but a few do after appropriate disclaimers. Interestingly enough, Maggie Kimmel, Professor at the University of Pittsburgh's library school and former President of ALSC (who describes herself as "far better at following up on projects than creating them, good at detail"), in response to the greatest strength question, says, "I think that I really do have the ability to inspire. . . . I can catch the attention and imagination of people and challenge them intellectually."

In *The Situational Leader*, Paul Hersey makes the point that personal power comes not only from the extent to which followers identify with the leader's goals; it also must be earned from the followers (p. 80). Hersey talks about three sources of personal power (pp. 80–81):

1. expertise, knowledge, skills of the leader
2. information power (leader has information, followers need access)
3. referent power (listening skills, strong interpersonal relationships)

Hersey compares personal power with position power (authority to punish, reward influential connections, etc.) and concludes that both kinds of power are important and both should be used by the leaders, depending on the situation.

Many of our library leaders recognize the limitations of position power and lean heavily on developing positive relationships with followers (staff). A few are strong advocates of situational leadership. Beverly Lynch notes that her research made her understand that her leadership style should vary depending on the situation.

> My work for four years at ACRL led people to think that I was not a forceful personality . . . that I was very amenable to the wishes of the membership and made sure their wishes were carried out; that I wrote letters for their signature, and when somebody said, "Didn't so-and-so send a great letter?" I would say, "Yes, terrific." The compulsion to say "Oh, yes, I wrote it" was completely suppressed. When I moved to the University of Illinois at Chicago, they thought of me as being very soft spoken and mild mannered . . . and my style changed completely. I was confrontational in the Mayor Daley mode because the situation called for it.

Lynch notes, "If I move again, we will see whether I can adapt to yet another environment." She goes on to say that she had wonderful job satisfaction both at ACRL and at the University of Illinois–Chicago because it has to be an internal satisfaction. "I don't have to have someone tell me that I did a great job if I know that I did." Lynch's self-confidence translates into adaptability.

Elizabeth Crabb, Director of the Northeast Texas Library System and an acknowledged mover-and-shaker in library development, says:

> My biggest strengths? Lord, do I have any big strengths? I think as I have grown older and gotten more experienced, I may have developed some leadership qualities and maybe a certain amount of charisma in that I can encourage people to great effort.

When asked to define charisma, Crabb said:

> Well, to me, it's like when they talk about Dukakis—he may have technocratic leadership ability, but he has difficulty being flippant or funny . . . and I can be serious and still make people enjoy it . . . at least that's what I try to do.

Crabb has recognized that her "charisma" comes not totally from within, but because her colleagues react positively to her approach. What our leaders all seem to understand is that sometimes these strengths, like "charisma" and "lack of fear," work very well; in other situations, they are not very successful; *but* overall the leaders' positive self-regard never wavers.

So along with broad vision and ability to motivate staff, our leaders have great faith in themselves. In many cases, this faith is acquired early in life, or at least early in their careers. Almost always, as we shall see in the following chapter, they attribute their success to the timely influence of another person.

Bennis and Nanus in *Leaders* say that positive self-regard has "three major components: knowledge of one's strengths, the capacity to nurture and develop those strengths, and the ability to discern the fit between one's strengths and weaknesses and the organization's needs" (p. 62).

For the most part, the library leaders are quick to describe their own strengths, but they do not talk at length about a phenomenon that Bennis is very excited about—the fact that leaders are perpetual learners. Some, he says, are "voracious readers"; others learn mainly from other people. Not surprisingly, our library leaders do not often talk about their reading habits. With the exception of Gary Strong, who says "I study constantly," they do not describe their excitement at learning new ways of accomplishing their work. It seems likely, however, that for most of the leaders, this aspect of their character is totally ingrained and it was taken for granted that the interviewer would understand this.

Our library leaders do read, but our conversations reveal that they have also been profoundly influenced by interaction with others in the field. The following chapter will describe in depth the way in which library leaders network and the people in our field who have had great impact on their careers.

REFERENCES

Bennis, Warren and Bert Nanus. Leaders: *The Strategies for Taking Charge*. New York: Harper, 1985.
Hersey, Paul. *The Situational Leader*. New York: Warner, 1985.

5
MENTORS, NETWORKING, AND ROLE MODELS IN LIBRARIANSHIP

It was exciting to be in library school and in Illinois at a time when the library community was whipped up to a fever pitch, with Al Trezza and all of the library development people. . . . I think Peggy Sullivan was one of the biggest influences on me in that I just loved watching her, and she let me do a few things that I thought were very kind. . . . I mean, I wrote a book with her while she was ALA President.

Kathleen Heim, Graduate Dean
Louisiana State University–Baton Rouge

Increasingly, in all professions, there is a growing awareness that the presence of mentors and role models can be a critical factor in one's career. What may not be quite so readily understood is that mentors are as important in attaining a senior position as they are in a first job and in middle management. In this chapter, our leaders describe their mentor-mentee and peer network experiences. The library leaders are quick to recognize a personal obligation to be role models for a new generation, but they also know that the relationship is a special one, and not everyone can be their mentee. Leaders spot and seek out potential leaders, but they also understand that part of their role is to encourage mentees to move off in their own direction. Our leaders detail how mentors behave in pulling people along, demanding the best, and providing opportunities both on the job and in professional organizations. They also describe disadvantages of hooking one's wagon to a "star" and the advantages of a large network.

Our library leaders talk expansively about the importance of mentors in their careers. They define mentor as a person who takes an exceptionally strong interest in the professional development of the mentee. Very often (but not always), the mentor is an established and recognized authority or leader in the field and is therefore able to provide sound advice and perspective, as well as important contacts, letters of reference, and so on.

The leaders remember their mentors with much more than a casual reference to their influence. Very often, intense admiration and gratitude are expressed. Our leaders make a clear distinction between mentors, role models, and peer networks. Only one or two of the leaders interviewed say that they have never had a mentor, but all readily cite examples of role models and (more frequently) helpful peers with whom they are quite consistently in touch.

Sometimes the role model is simply a person that our leaders have read about, have heard speak at a meeting, or have followed his or her publications. Unlike the mentoring relationships, our leaders often have little or no contact with their role models and, in one or two cases, note that the role model "probably never knew I existed."

Library leaders well understand the importance of mentoring in its varied aspects and recognize their obligation to be role models for the next generation of leaders. Some, like Penny Abell, feel quite strongly about it.

> We better stop being so negative and we'd better start
> being a whole lot more concerned again about the kind
> of developmental experience, and the kind of modeling
> we are doing, and the kind of opportunities that we are
> giving people to demonstrate their abilities to lead.

Abell says it is extremely important to "articulate a level of expectation and a sense of direction for staff."

Richard Dougherty calls for more recognition of leadership and is critical of the profession in this regard.

We seem to revel in people's failures; we speculate about why somebody is having trouble or got ousted, but we do very little in terms of honoring those who have been successful. This profession needs successes, as many as possible. We'll all benefit, bask in the successes.

Networking

Over and over again, the library leaders say that right out of library school, and very often while in school, they were advised, they were pushed, they were offered positions. With almost no exceptions, all of those interviewed say they had mentors early in their careers. They have no trouble naming them. Many are still in touch with their early mentors. Those few who could not identify mentors had networks—colleagues throughout the country whom they call and who call them to exchange news, ask advice, and keep attuned to the profession's grapevine. Sometimes these calls are made only once or twice a year, or they meet these friends only at conferences, but the bonds are strong.

Only Beverly Lynch sounds a small note of caution about this. She says, "The most successful librarians are those who interact with their environment. The least successful are those who only talk to each other." Lynch, however, is quick to admit that she has had her own mentors and now has a small network of confidantes.

Most of the leaders are concerned about the future of the profession and seek to identify those with leadership potential. Richard Dougherty says, "I do have a talent for building staffs and getting people to work and develop; I really enjoy that. I have about thirteen people who have worked for me who are now ARL directors; they worked for me as assistants or associates."

Dougherty says he was strongly influenced by Ralph Shaw of Rutgers, Jerrold Orne of the University of North Carolina–Chapel Hill, and several others in his early career. "They had a significant influence on me because they let me do things and let me make mistakes, and once in a while they would bring me in and give me some advice." Apparently, Dougherty's early mentors may have also instilled in him the importance of mentoring others, and perhaps the importance of networking, because of the many names mentioned by other leaders in discussing persons who have influenced their careers, Dougherty's name surfaced over and over again. Russell Shank's comment is typical.

> I've never had any mentors; I've had a lot of people I've learned from. . . . As it turns out, we talk about things that interest me. I'm able to ask, to expose my thoughts, my problems, my concerns, and they have things to say about them. . . . Dick Dougherty is one; he's not a mentor, but you can pick up a conversation almost any time, in a beer hall, or over the phone, and we stood one night until 4 o'clock in the morning at the Oklahoma Library Association. . . . It was something about a networking operation with the Research Libraries Group, and I didn't see the reason for it, the need for it, and we went back and forth and got pretty heated, but it was fun.

Shank contrasts Dougherty's style with others who, when an issue is broached, just say, "Oh, yeah, well that probably is a problem and walk away."

While many mentors are found on the job, the significance of conferences or professional committee work cannot be overemphasized. Many of these contacts are made somewhat serendipitously, but develop into life-long relationships. A case in point occurred at the author's second ALA conference in Kansas City, 1968. As a fledgling library development staff member in New Mexico, somewhat with trepidation she approached Joe Shubert (then State Librarian of Ohio) with a question about consulting. Forty-five minutes of conversation later, she had a mini-course in library development issues and trends and the beginnings of a career-long friendship. Obviously, association leaders are often too busy for long conversations, but their interest in and concern for newcomers to the profession, combined with a natural enthusiasm for their work, make such encounters possible and even probable.

More frequently, professional association leaders become interested in new professionals because of their creativity, reliability, productivity, persistence, and overall contribution to the work of the group. Many volunteer, but only a few are motivated and highly productive. Leaders constantly seek out new talent, not only for association work, but also for their own staffs. One common thread is apparent in talking with the leaders: their mentor or role model emerged early in their careers. Frequently, they were identified as having leadership potential, if not in library school, then on their first job. The implication here is that every job, even the very first, is important.

Mentoring, or something akin to mentoring, is generational; that is, mentoring links generations of leaders. Russell Shank gives a good example of how this works.

> Bob Leigh [Robert D. Leigh], the former Dean of the library school at Columbia, was in a quiet way very influential, again not a mentor, but the kind of thoughtful person who would right away hone in on your problem almost as a father figure. When I was working at Columbia, he wanted me to teach once a year in the library school; he did not call me up or ask me to come to the library school. He wandered into my office one day. He was a former President of Bennington College and one of the big men in newspaper analysis, but essentially he was just a kind person with a great insight for people. He never offended anybody, but he was just able to pull you along.

In turn, Elaine Sloan represents the third generation of mentees in the Leigh-Shank chain. While a Ph.D. student at the University of Maryland with no library experience, Sloan was provided the opportunity to intern with Russell Shank, then Librarian at the Smithsonian. Shank immediately took her under his wing, and she left the Smithsonian in 1977 to become Associate University Librarian at Berkeley. Sloan says, "I guess that I was one of the first of the old boys that wasn't an old boy."

Another example of the passing of the mantle is Pat Woodrum and the late Allie Beth Martin (formerly Director of the Tulsa City-County Library System and ALA President in 1975–76). Woodrum recalls:

> Allie Beth was very instrumental in my development as a librarian, and there were two qualities we all admired. One, she was a very political animal and she knew how to work the system; and the second was her ability to cause you to be enthusiastic about a project or job that you really didn't want to do. You could go into her office, and she'd give you an assignment, and you could hardly wait to get out and get started, and then you'd leave the office and think, "I didn't want to do that."

Recognizing Talent

Linda Crismond says that her management style was developed by two mentors—Marty Martell, then Assistant Director of the San Francisco Public Library, and Roy Kidman, Director of the University of Southern California Library.

> Martell offered me the choice of two special projects— one was to automate the library, the other was to establish the Bay Area Reference Center. I chose the automation and ended up developing the first serials control system in a public library in the U.S. He gave me the opportunity and then he let me alone, but made me make sure that I was responsive to the direction he wanted to go . . . and that gave me high visibility, that gave me the confidence, and it also gave me the ease to work with top administration, which, as a new librarian, a young librarian, I would not have had. . . .
>
> And when I moved to USC and I was still in my twenties, Kidman rounded out the management style. He always asked the questions, "Well, so what?" "Who cares?" "What is the significance of what you are say-

ing?" "What is your recommendation?" "Don't just list a bunch of facts and resources." He kept forcing it, and I can remember that sometimes I'd get so mad at him. I would do all this work, and then he wouldn't like it; and he'd send me back to do more . . . and he would keep doing that until he got me to the point where I could anticipate what he wanted and do it right the first time, do it completely the first time. . . . He wanted me to do all the background, think through what I was doing, put it in the proper context, *and* make the recommendation.

Toni Bearman talks about her experiences as a Library Assistant at the Brown University library. At this point, Bearman did not have a college degree, but she was hired by Louis Vagianos and put in charge of the public services area of a large branch.

We were planning a new science library. I looked at the plans and had some concerns about the layout. I told my boss. The next day, in comes Mr. Vagianos with the floor plan to ask why I didn't like it. I started telling him. He liked my points. He put faith in me and decided I was a young person worth encouraging. He spent time helping me learn to think. That had a tremendous impact on how I felt managers should act and what their responsibilities should be.

Barbara Immroth, the University of Texas at Austin, tells a similar story about Vagianos (now at Dalhousie). When she was a senior at Brown, he talked with her about careers in libraries and suggested library schools.

Tom Galvin describes three important mentors and role models in his career. The first and primary mentor was Kenneth Shaffer, former Dean of Simmons College library school, who

gave me an opportunity to teach when I'd been out of school [with an MLS] less than a year. . . . it never occurred to me that I could direct a library [Marblehead

Public] when I was 24 years old, but Ken persuaded me
that I could. . . . I think this was a critical decision point
in my career because I've always been persuaded by the
correctness of Ken Shaffer's view, which is that the
biggest jump you make in your career as a manager is
when you go from being in a subordinate position to
being in the position where you are responsible for the
entire operation. It doesn't matter what size the operation is. . . . it was Ken's view that the earlier in your career that you made that jump, the more successful you
would be.

Galvin says that Shaffer and Jesse Shera were the two dominant role models, but the mentoring was quite different.

In Ken's case, it was quite conscious. When we went to
a professional meeting, Ken would sit me down in ad-
vance of the meeting, tell me who I should meet, see to
it that I got to meet those people. I was on a first-name
basis with people who were ten to twenty years older
than I was very early in my career.
    Shera, on the other hand, was never a mentor in that
sense. If anybody had suggested to Jesse that he should
feel any responsibility for my career, he would have
thought that was ridiculous although he did do that for
other people. . . . I went to [Case Western] Reserve because Jesse was there, but I would not have had the
nerve to ask him to be my major advisor because he had
never been one, and physically it was so difficult for him
to do anything with a dissertation. He couldn't read any
manuscripts, but he asked to be my major advisor after I
had the dissertation well in progress.

Galvin notes that neither Shera nor Shaffer was an organization person; "they were critics . . . gadflies." His decisive mentor in ALA was Frances (Fanny) Neel Cheney, Professor at
George Peabody College, who got him his first committee ap-
pointment. In fact, several of the library leaders mentioned the

enormous influence of Cheney. Of these tributes, perhaps Ed Holley's is most eloquent.

> Fanny Cheney was unquestionably the finest teacher I ever had, at least in higher education . . . her reference and literature classes where she invited in all of her friends—the Dean of Engineering, the head of the political science department—to talk about the literature of their fields . . . her sense of humor, and the principles that she laid down . . . kind of offhand. I really owe that woman an enormous debt, which I have tried from time to time to repay in various ways. She probably had a lot to do with setting my philosophy about librarianship.

The dozens of examples of how our current leaders were singled out by their mentors leads us to the critical questions: What did the last generation of leaders find extraordinary about these people? What qualities did the young Crismond, Bearman, Galvin, and Holley have that warranted the investment of time and support? In what kind of setting can new talent be discovered?

Lacking an understanding of the motives of the individual mentors, it is safe to say that all four mentees (Crismond, Bearman, Galvin, and Holley) were endowed with high intelligence; all were ambitious; all were strong communicators; and all had a high energy level—an energy level that, translated into a mind-set, helped them tackle each new problem with both vigor and creativity.

But probably the single quality that most attracted Kidman, Vagianos, Shaffer, Shera, and others was, in its own way, a kind of chemistry, an open-mindedness on the part of these mentees that was rare, a high receptivity to the mentors' ideas. It seems safe to assume that these four leaders, as well as all others mentioned in this chapter, learned early in life the value of being an active listener.

As noted earlier in this chapter, the influence of library school professors on the careers of our leaders has been profound. Penny Abell talks about how she got into librarianship.

She was looking for a career she could pursue while following her husband as his job location changed.

> We found this flyer from SUNY–Albany, and my first two classes were with Vince Aceto and Mary Lee Bundy. . . . they were wonderful teachers. . . . Vince opened up this feeling of quest, that one is on a quest in this field . . . and Mary Lee Bundy was brilliant . . . and so I went to library school because it was going to be a convenient degree, and I was absolutely turned on with those two courses . . . and I had other courses later that were of the traditional and awful kind, but they never were enough to turn me off.

Kathleen Heim, who is a role model and mentor to many in this profession, says, "My good fortune at the University of Chicago was to fall under the influence of Lester Asheim, who made the difference for me. He was rigorous, and he made me write. . . . that activity of writing a thesis under Asheim was critical. It made the difference between my just going out and working, and going out and having a thoughtful career."

Jean Curtis went to library school at the University of Maryland after years of experience at the District of Columbia Public Library. At Maryland, she became the Graduate Assistant of Margaret Chisholm, then a faculty member, later Dean. Curtis says:

> She was such a dynamic force, and I just felt she was magnificent. She's always so enthusiastic, no matter what. We had a lot of positive conversations, and I know she doesn't remember that—just a brief encounter thing, but such an influence in my life. One thing Margaret let me do, she let me talk with classes a couple of times. She said, "Jean, would you talk about your experiences because these people really don't know; they want to know what the real world is like." And that was just a wonderful thing for me because the students really responded.

Recruitment

There are literally hundreds of anecdotes about library school faculty who have profoundly influenced the careers of their students. Perhaps one of the most important aspects of these stories is in the area of recruitment. Some have a talent for locating and nurturing those who have potential. One example is Blanche Woolls, Professor and former Chair of the library science department at the University of Pittsburgh, who identifies, and then persistently works with, the individual until he is enrolled, then on through the program. Woolls has been particularly successful at recruiting students into library education. Her former fellowship students (U.S. Department of Education Title IIB) occupy positions on library school faculties throughout the United States.

Woolls' role model for recruiting and nurturing students was the late Sarah Rebecca Reed, Dean at Emporia. Reed took a personal interest in her students; her philosophy was that an unhappy student could not succeed. Therefore, she made sure that students' social, financial, and emotional needs were also the school's concern.

Over and over again, our leaders provide anecdotal material about how library school faculty pushed, propelled them immediately into positions of substance. Bill Summers talks about Lowell Martin, then Dean at Rutgers, who gave him a job working with Ralph Blasingame (the Director of the Pennsylvania State Library) on the first Pennsylvania survey. Summers says "I had a new and growing family and needed money. . . . I did all the statistics on that survey, and I'll never forget, he paid me $100 a day. Wow! Unheard of wage in those days!" He continues:

> Ralph Blasingame had a lot to do, for example, with my becoming State Librarian of Florida since he had just done a study down there, and of course when I left my first job as librarian in Coco, Florida, my mentors helped because Providence, Rhode Island, was looking for an Assistant Director. They wrote the library school, and Lowell wrote back saying, "You know, Bill Summers is

one of the people you should consider," and then when they got my credentials, they said I didn't have enough experience. I guess Martin and Ralph Shaw [Professor at Rutgers] wrote them back and said, "We know he doesn't have a lot of experience, but we think he's got a lot of ability, and you ought to look at him anyhow." And they did, and they gave me the job. So it was those people sort of standing behind me that moved me along.

One of the great things about Rutgers in those days was that professors like Shaw, Martin, Mary Gaver, and Margaret Monroe drew a lot of people there, and this was in the days when recruiters used to come and visit. Shaw would always make us interview, go be interviewed, because he knew all these people, and I met Emerson Greenaway [Librarian at the Free Library of Philadelphia], and I met Milton Lord [Boston Public Library] and all kinds of people I wouldn't have met for years just coming into the profession.

Sometimes a minor incident early in a career can have a marked impact on a person's self-confidence. Duane Webster, Executive Director of the Association for Research Libraries, talks about an experience with Harold Hacker when Hacker was Director of the Rochester Public Library.

When I was resigning, he called me in and said, "Duane, I'm sorry you are leaving. . . . I want to name you as my special assistant. Will you stay and be my assistant?" This surprised me because I did not work directly with him; I was down in the bowels of the organization. Even though I had made up my mind to leave, this was a great encouragement.

Webster goes on to say that one of the keys to his success at ARL has been a series of mentors: Warren (Jim) Haas, Steve McCarthy (Cornell), and Fred Cole (formerly Director, Council on Library Resources). He speaks particularly about Jim Haas.

I've been a Jim Haas student; that is to say, I've looked at what he has been doing, thought about what he has been doing, worked hand in glove with him, and I've worked at some distance from him. . . . his ideas, his conceptual outlook are just very important.

Webster speaks of others who have been helpful to him at ARL.

Page Ackerman, gem of a person, absolutely magnificent, very sage advice, very thoughtful, very caring. And Bob Vosper, her predecessor at UCLA, has to this day continued to take an interest. . . . Herman Fussler [University of Chicago], Foster Mohrhardt [CLR]. . . and then following those folks there was another generation that came through—John McDonald [University of Connecticut], Jay Lucker [MIT], Dick DeGennero. . . . all have a magnificent ability to contribute . . . and I count on them to this moment for advice and counsel.

Webster goes on to talk about and praise current management committee members for their ability to say, "How can we help you?"

When Maggie Kimmel was asked about her mentors, she said:

Well, different people at different times. Gary Public Library staff, a history teacher, my major professor in college, Sister Alberta Smogness. She was a Dominican . . . told me I was a born teacher, and when I went into the library, she said, "Libraries are central to the teaching process!" People at the Pratt Library were very influential . . . also Isabella Jinette [Enoch Pratt Library] and Augusta Baker [New York Public Library] . . . Carolyn Field [Free Library of Philadelphia] . . . but in that beginning period, the person that I thought the most of, who has had a continuing but very different influence on me, is Peggy Sullivan [now Director of Libraries, Northern Illinois University]. She was my ideal. She had been at the Pratt Library before I was, and actually had the job that I had when I left, as Assistant Coordinator. She had the qualities I admired—her broad professional perspective, the fact that she was a practitioner and teacher—that she knew people from children's services, but that she had also broadened out.

Sometimes, a few rather casual comments can make a decided difference in one's career. Mary Lankford says:

When I took this job [referring to her current position, Coordinator of Library and Media Services, Irving, Texas, Public Schools], the man who hired me had just written a federal proposal for Chapter I funds . . . and he said, "Do you realize what you will be doing?" I didn't know what the federal program was; I had no idea. He said, "You will be establishing libraries; you will have to set procedures, and these will have long-range effects." And he really wanted me to realize the magnitude of what I was about. . . . He would come in and talk to me, and he [a curriculum director] was a member of ALA. He said, "Why aren't you an ALA member? You'll gain by it." So I joined ALA then, that year. . . . He forced me into a wider vision—into looking beyond, into tomorrow.

Lee Brawner talks about his start in Dallas in young adult services "under the tutelage of an absolute tyrant of a Young Adult Coordinator, Ray Fry, who of course bounded on to other luminary positions—a gentle tyrant, the best teacher you could want. He asked a lot, expected a lot, and liberally quizzed you on your reading assignments."

Clearly, mentoring is alive and well in the library profession. In the past, when most major library positions were held by men, the old boy network was obviously alive and well. Most of the male leaders interviewed were quickly pushed into positions of responsibility by male library school faculty or male library directors. Now, in the nineties, when the ratio of female to male library administrators more closely approximates the demographics of our profession, it would be interesting to see if similar patterns prevail in upward mobility patterns for women.

We do know that many women in leadership roles work hard to bring others along. Patricia Schuman, interviewed while she was ALA Treasurer, noted that she has never considered herself a leader, has "always been pushed by others, and when I work with people, I always try to get new people involved, always try to get them to replace me."

Several of the interviewees discuss the importance of a mentor at critical points in their careers. Ching-chih Chen, Professor and Associate Dean at Simmons College's library school, says that she asked Tom Galvin (who was then at Simmons) to read and critique her first article, and "he literally tore it apart, but that help and support made a very great difference to me." Similarly, Leigh Estabrook, now Dean of the University of Illinois' library school, says that earlier in her career, when she urgently needed a job, she called Galvin, and within hours he arranged for her to meet the person who subsequently hired her.

The Mentor's Personality

How does one become a mentor, a role model, or an effective node in a network? It has much to do with demeanor and personality. Bob Warner talks about meeting Peter Drucker when they both were given honorary degrees by DePauw University. Warner says of Drucker: "Nice guy . . . these really big people are very honest, very approachable, not phony, not stuffed shirts, and so on. . . . Very nice people. It's always fun to deal with the big people I've found in life."

Most of the leaders in our field are natural mentors. They understand that a mentor-mentee relationship must naturally evolve and that such relationships do not last forever. The mentor has to be willing to spend time with the mentee . . . take time at conferences to introduce the mentee to others who can be of help . . . give objective advice and criticism. Jennifer Cargill says, in an article in *Library Administration and Management:*

The ideal is that mentor and mentee move toward establishing a peer relationship in which there is graceful acceptance of the fact that the protegé may progress further in a career path than the mentor did. The secure mentor will enjoy this. . . . The protegé should begin identifying people that he or she can assist and should utilize the former mentor as a participant in this new mentor, protegé relationship [p. 14].

Finding a mentor is not always that easy. The kind of mentoring experience that Heim had with Asheim or that Holley had with Cheney does not happen with every library science student. It does not happen with fifty percent of our students. How, then, and where does the new and ambitious professional find mentors? Naturally, the highly visible leaders are sought after, but they may have very little time and very little in common with the would-be protegé. There is also the danger of achieving certain recognition primarily because of close association with someone holding a prominent position in an association, an organization, or both. When that person leaves the organization or loses power, as inevitably occurs, the protegé will be alone, and the wise mentor will make certain that his or her protegés are not viewed as handmaidens or shills. The leaders of today have continuing responsibility to ensure that there emerges a continuing wave of new leaders.

Potential mentors are available at all levels of the organization. "Leaders" are available at all levels of the organization. The library science student will recognize them because they love their work, they believe that what they are doing is important, they are results-oriented, and they achieve remarkable standards of service. Depending on the size of the organization, there may be several potential mentors. The person who can best help improve one's skills—the teacher or coach—is not necessarily the person who gives career advice and makes contacts for the mentor. The person who opens doors is not necessarily the protector—the person who rescues a fledgling library professional from making mistakes. Developing a rather wide network of professional friends, both in one's own locale and nationally, is the best way to ensure that career help, advice, and encouragement will be readily available.

Bennis says, in *On Becoming a Leader*, "I know of no leader in any era who hasn't had at least one mentor: a teacher who found things in him he didn't know were there, a parent, a senior associate who showed him the way to be, or in some cases not to be, or demanded more from him than he knew he had to give" (p. 91).

REFERENCES

Bennis, Warren. *On Becoming a Leader*. Reading Mass.: Addison-Wesley, 1989.

Cargill, Jennifer. "Developing Library Leaders: The Role of Mentorship." *Library Administration and Management* (Winter 1989).

6

DEVELOPING LEADERS:
Implications for Library Education

Library school deans need to bite the bullet, seek out the potential leaders . . . subject them to rigor . . . statistics, problem solving, and, yes, an understanding of the nature of leadership.

Anne Mathews
Director of Library Programs
U.S. Department of Education

Why haven't our professional schools, specifically schools of library and information science, done more to address the questions of how we can attract those with potential for leadership, and how we can educate them for leadership positions? We often respond passively to this issue, yet we bear significant responsibility for educating the leaders of tomorrow. June Lester, in her article in *Leadership for Research Libraries,* says:

> The degree to which the library and information science education community as a whole has given conscious attention to the need to educate for leadership, especially within the parameters of the master's level program, is almost imperceptible, if one bases such measurement on the published literature [p. 131].

Lester also notes that education for leadership has not been a major concern in conferences "where library school deans have grappled with questions of improving the educational product." There is also no indication that schools with two-year master's programs are strengthening their focus on leadership development.

However, this is not to say that education for leadership is not taking place in our professional schools. Again, quoting Lester, it "occurs in strange and wonderful ways. Sometimes it occurs by design, sometimes by example, sometimes by accident, sometimes by serendipity, sometimes not at all." The point is that we can probably do better than a serendipitous approach, and we owe it to our students and to our profession to do better.

If leading graduate schools of management are now recognizing the need for increased emphasis on leadership skills, then schools of library and information studies can and should absorb these principles into their management education. We have, in our management classes, adopted a traditional definition of management as the science (or perhaps the art) of getting things done. In fact, management encompasses a much more sensitive process of dealing with people, issues, and ideas in highly complex environments.

The neglect of leadership issues is due primarily to the fact that leadership and related issues have not been studied in any concerted way by our profession, nor have leadership concepts been integrated into the mainstream of library and information science education. Many feel that such a topic has little place and importance for our students, and thus there is no room in or outside the curriculum.

It is premature, without further research, to outline a definitive model curriculum, but this chapter discusses the status of and need for research, cites the distinctions between management and leadership, and describes some components of leadership education that could and should be integrated into the master's program.

John Gardner tells us quite correctly in *Leadership Papers* that "we cannot expect our graduate and professional schools to send their graduates out with all their future greatness prepackaged." But he also warns that "our educational systems rather than igniting enthusiasm for leadership may well snuff it out. Far from encouraging them, it will very likely persuade them that what society needs are experts and professionals, not leaders. Professional people often sound—perhaps without intending it—as though they would prefer a world in which there are no leaders—only experts" (pp. 76–77).

In a 1985 study commissioned by the Office of Library Personnel Resources of the American Library Association, slightly less than half of all respondents agreed that the training they received was good preparation for work they were doing. The senior management group was least satisfied with its library school training in terms of preparation for current positions. Computer and technology training and management development training were most frequently mentioned as areas in which professional development is needed. The need for interpersonal skills training and for subject training (science, business, language, etc.) was noted by 20 percent of the total sample. The need for interpersonal skill training increased in importance with each succeeding seniority group (see Bernstein and Leach, *Developing Leadership Skills*, in References at the end of this chapter).

It could be argued that the professional schools basically educate students to assume entry-level positions, and cannot be expected to anticipate the leadership challenges inherent in more responsible positions. The reality is, however, as has been emphasized in earlier chapters, that opportunities to exercise leadership abound at every level of the library organization. As noted by Lester:

> Although the tendency is to think of leaders as those who have rank or authority or high position, the leaders in our field have also been the thinkers, the ones who challenged the status quo, the developers of new approaches and ways of conceptualizing what we do. They have been the individual librarians, unknown and unsung outside of a specific environment [p. 144].

Current leadership theory, the interviews with library leaders, and this author's experiences in library education have all combined to profoundly convince her that all of our students have some measure of (admittedly often latent) leadership ability, and this ability can be identified, nurtured, and strengthened in the process of attaining the first professional degree. As Bennis says in *Leaders*, "Leadership seems to be the marshalling of skills possessed by a majority but used by a minority. But it is something that can be learned by everyone, taught to everyone, denied to no one" (p. 27).

James Kouzes and Barry Posner make the point that no one ever questions whether managers are born or made.

> Why should management be viewed as a set of skills and abilities, but leadership be seen as a set of innate personality characteristics? We have simply assumed that management can be taught. . . . the same can be done with leadership. By viewing leadership as a nonlearnable set of character traits, a self-fulfilling prophecy has been created that dooms societies to having only a few good leaders. If you assume that leadership is learnable, you will be surprised to discover how many good leaders there really are [p. 314].

Librarians and information professionals are needed who are prepared and positioned so that they can influence the character of institutions. If libraries are to be fully recognized as agencies essential to the cultural, educational, and economic life of their communities, then they must be staffed with leaders who can reorganize, renew, and redirect resources with vigor and assurance. It is a small indicator, but a positive one, that in the (proposed) new ALA standards for the accreditation of schools of library and information studies, the section on curriculum notes, "The curriculum fosters development of library and information professionals who will assume an assertive role in providing services."

While the curriculum is the obvious place to start in considering the problem of developing leadership potential, there are several other areas that can be strengthened to build the kind of environment in our professional schools that identifies and nurtures leadership, so that by the time our students graduate, they not only have their first jobs, but also self-esteem, self-confidence, and the solid beginnings of a network that will serve them well as they move along in their careers.

There are at least five distinct areas in which schools of library and information studies have a major role to play in the understanding of leadership and the development of leaders: research, recruitment, curriculum, mentoring, and career planning. In the previous chapter, Richard Dougherty was quoted on the need to recognize those who have been successful in our profession. Although our students do read and hear about the legendary figures in our field—such heroes as Melvil Dewey, Jesse Shera, Fred Kilgore, Henriette Avram, Larry Powell—but at the same time, one of the most widely cited articles on the subject of leadership in the profession is entitled, "Oh, Where Have All the Leaders Gone?" In it, the author, Herbert White, observes that "leadership, much as we admire it in the abstract, is something we suspect in the specific."

Perhaps this attitude explains why relatively little research has been done on the nature of leadership in the library and information professions. Except for biographical studies, which by no means should be discounted, research on leadership in our field did not begin until recently, and it has largely centered around the following questions: Who are the perceived leaders? To what degree is the meaning of the term *leadership* shared throughout our field? Do those who are perceived as leaders share similar patterns of background, behavior, and career experiences? To what extent do publishing and participation in professional organizations relate to perceived leadership? (Gertzog, 1986).

Other studies have been done on the behavior of library directors and its effect on the organizational effectiveness of the library (see, for example, the article by Euster); leadership styles and rate of change in public libraries (see the dissertation by Boyd); and discrepancies between the leaders' self-perceptions and the perceptions of their subordinates (see the dissertations and article by Dragon, Rike, and Sparks). Bandelin's dissertation in progress at Texas Woman's University uses citation analysis to examine the nature of the publication records of Gerzog's 115 leaders.

Richard Dougherty asserts that we need to know more

about our leaders; we also need to know more about the nature of leadership in our field. Greater understanding of how our leaders successfully cope with change and their risk-taking and decision-making behaviors would not only enable educators to do a better job of recruitment, but also enable them to design better leadership development programs as part of library education. Knowledge of what factors led our most brilliant and successful leaders into the information professions also would be helpful in recruitment. And a more definitive understanding of qualities needed to be successful in this field would help admissions committees identify the most promising applicants. It is apparent that as applications soar and our schools grow more crowded, simply continuing to raise numerical standards for the GRE and GPA will not necessarily recruit individuals with potential to succeed in rapidly changing information environments.

The profession has been challenged to find and preserve the "wild ducks" (White, p. 69), those individuals who ask the difficult questions, who are not afraid to buck the system, who stand on principle no matter how great the cost. In recruitment efforts, our schools should make certain that these wild ducks are not culled out. It is crucial that we recognize the importance of individuality and that we bring into our profession not only persons who hold unique perspectives, but also those who stand up for their beliefs.

Having recruited these paragons, can the schools then provide—both inside and outside the curriculum—elements that will nurture and develop leadership skills? It is certain that some of these elements already exist, but part of the problem has been articulated as "an outmoded concept of the appropriate role of librarians to be implementors and followers rather than creators and leaders" (see the article by Battin).

Most master's programs require a course in basic management and additional courses in various types of library administration, as well as the occasional specialized course in personnel management, fiscal management, communications (interpersonal and group dynamics), and so on. Most of the core management courses at least touch on leadership skills, and certainly there is overlap between management and leadership, but generally the focus is on such traditional elements of management as planning, organizing, staffing, directing, controlling, and measuring library effectiveness.

Students need to know all of the above, but if the approach is linear, relies heavily on technical skills for solving problems, and sidesteps the essential behavioral attributes needed, then we are not producing graduates who are knowledgeable about their own strengths and weaknesses and who have a strong set of personal values and beliefs. Bennis, in *Leaders*, makes the point that "most management education makes certain assumptions that are dangerously misleading—namely that the goals are clear, alternatives known, technology and its consequences certain, and perfect information available" (p. 221).

Rather, we should be teaching our students the distinctions between leadership and management. Again, Bennis, in *On Becoming a Leader*, makes a plea for teaching students to be innovators rather than administrators; to focus on people rather than systems and structures; to have their eyes on the horizon rather than the bottom line; to challenge the status quo rather than accept it; and, finally, to "do the right thing" rather than "do things right."

In Donald Riggs's volume of essays on library leadership (*Library Leadership: Visualizing the Future*), Michael Gorman writes:

> The essential differences between management/administration on the one hand and leadership on the other are that the former is concerned with what is and the latter is concerned with what will be. One accepts the *status quo* (and often yearns for the *status quo ante*); the other dares to imagine and to create the future. In technical services, the manager/administrator strives to make the returns of the current system as great as possible, whereas the leader seeks better alternatives to the current system [p. 74].

As Richard Budd, Dean at Rutgers, expresses it, "The goal of education is to prepare students for their *last* job rather than their first—to put them in a position where they will continue to prepare themselves for upper-level jobs." Both managers and leaders are needed, but library education should not continue the status quo, that is, educating students to make things run smoothly, control people and resources. We must also prepare them for creative, highly proactive roles.

Kouzes and Posner, in *The Leadership Challenge,* note that "traditional management teaching would have us believe that the ideal organization is orderly and stable. Yet when successful leaders talk about their personal best achievements, they talk about challenging the process, about changing things, about shaking up the organization" (p. xvi).

As noted in the introduction, the library leaders interviewed are in tune with current management trends; they have been among the first to shift away from a somewhat mechanical model of planning and efficiency focused primarily on assessing needs, setting goals, and so forth. The new approaches do not throw out the systematic approach, but they place much more emphasis on creativity, risk taking, innovation, and even intuition. As Kouzes finds in his study of the corporate sector, this author finds the library leaders generally to be almost the opposite of cool, aloof, and analytical; rather, they are passionate, intense, caring, and kind. How can our professional schools foster these elusive leadership qualities? Certainly, it cannot be done by simply adding new courses to an already crowded curriculum.

The following curriculum elements and suggestions for creating an environment that fosters leadership development have evolved from this author's interviews with the library leaders; work with the ALA Task Force on Leadership (appointed by Margaret Chisholm in 1987); subsequent work on the curriculum for the first Snowbird Leadership Institute (August 1990), organized by Dennis Day of the Salt Lake City Public Library, and funded by Dynix; observations from her management classes; suggestions from her doctoral issues seminar participants and other colleagues at Texas Woman's University; and, of course, conversations with practitioners at many levels of the library organization, in many different types of libraries.

As Lester points out in her article in *Leadership for Research Libraries,* many of the accredited library schools state in their goals and objectives that they seek either to be leaders in advancing the profession (through instruction, research, and service) or to educate librarians who will assume leadership roles in the profession. The latter goal should translate into a specific program to identify and recruit potential leaders and to provide specific opportunities throughout the professional education to develop and improve leadership skills. Along with identification and training, the school should consciously create an environment where mentoring relationships can and do develop readily, and foster various kinds of networks to support career advancement.

This section focuses on curriculum, with possible application to the basic course in management, which is required at most library schools. Perhaps this focus on leadership might as easily be accomplished in an elective course, in a series of one-hour courses interspersed throughout the master's program, or outside the structured degree environment.

Assuming that one or more of these options are available, how does one begin? First of all, it is generally agreed that the most important aspect of leadership training is the opportunity to gain specific knowledge of one's own strengths and weaknesses. Understanding and accepting oneself are basic goals. Therefore, it is suggested that students in the management course (or in another structured learning situation) take such tests as Myer-Briggs, Strong Campbell Interest Inventory, or California Psychological Inventory and other shorter tests that evaluate personality, propensity for risk taking, and other attitudes. The first sessions would be spent with students analyzing the results of the tests. (This approach presupposes that the instructor of management has or will attain skill and experience in analyzing the results of such tests.)*

As the instructor moves into management and leadership concepts, students who have achieved an awareness of their own strengths and weaknesses will have a different perspective than those who are simply examining a theory in the abstract. They will be involved in evaluating their own style in relation to the principles and practices of management and

*At the Center for Creative Leadership in Greensboro, North Carolina, all institutes begin with self-assessment, and the results are applied throughout the sessions to help participants relate concepts to their own style of leadership.

leadership. As the course proceeds, students should have the opportunity to synthesize (using experiential as well as traditional methods) their style of leadership with effective models of leadership. Ideally, after the self-assessments are completed, students will have the opportunity to choose areas of study and activity that are particularly relevant to areas they wish to enhance or strengthen.

Some of these qualities we hope to develop may include:

The ability to develop and share with others a vision that extends beyond immediate concerns; an understanding of the difference between strategic planning and visionary leadership.

An understanding of how change occurs and affects the immediate environment; an understanding of how to create and initiate change.

An understanding of risk taking as it relates to leadership vis-à-vis management (i.e., the ability to make decisions in the absence of full information).

An understanding of the positive uses of power.

Skills in conflict management.

Skills in communicating, negotiating, clarifying, and recommending policy options.

Sensitivity and perspective toward the complex problems library organizations face in the context of their political environments.

The development of a strong ideological commitment and sense of professional ethics. Social responsibility; the capacity to take global view and move away from short-term bottom-line thinking; to become actively engaged in long-term planning for the betterment of society.

The ability to lead as well as follow and to engender broad support for the issues that affect our profession.

A desirable component of the program is the availability of internships with practitioners who are in leadership positions (at various levels) and in situations where students' skills can be refined and tested. At minimum, students should be provided opportunities to meet and interact with leaders in our field. A final major component of a course (or a preliminary activity before graduation) would be an introspective analysis of the students' leadership style, accompanied by a self-development plan for improvement of leadership skills.

It does not matter much whether these and similar concepts are presented in one course, interspersed throughout courses in various ways or presented outside the degree program. What is important is that new students are quickly welcomed to an academic environment that is alive with high expectations and that by graduation, students will be self-confident and well prepared to assume a leadership role in whatever organization they join and at whatever level they are placed.

Clearly, one course, or even a series of courses, will not fully accomplish these objectives. The various attributes of leadership cannot be assigned to a list of measurable learning objectives and transferred into the mind of the unsuspecting master's student. However, we can at least teach students the difference between management and leadership skills. We can build their self-esteem; we can offer discussion and practice in leadership principles, and we can consciously socialize our students into the profession by introducing them to leaders in practice.

Library educators can assume a key role in developing leadership for the library and information professions. This process begins in the dean's office. The dean, as leader of leaders, must demonstrate that students are central to our work. They are our most valuable "product." This attitude toward students must permeate the organization. Educators sometimes whine that they are not rewarded for attention to students, and on one level that is true; in academia today, it is research that brings respect and rewards. On the other hand, the real *satisfaction* that leaders in library education express about their work focuses on the growth, development, and achievements of their students.

Our schools of library and information studies should create a leadership culture. Institutionalizing the concept means more than providing education for leadership; it means rewarding faculty for helping to institutionalize that culture and recognizing them for their success in mentoring students, in helping graduates form their own network of relationships during graduate school and also as they move forward in their careers.

When students recognize that they are not just numbers, that there is genuine concern for them as individuals on the part of administration and faculty, and that close attention is being paid not only to their technical skills, but also to their socialization into the profession, their self-confidence grows, and their ambitions soar. Ultimately, the profession is enriched.

REFERENCES

Bandelin, Janice M. "Publishing Characteristics of Perceived Library Leaders." Dissertation in progress, Texas Woman's University.

Battin, Patricia. "Developing University and Research Library Professionals." *American Libraries* 14 (January 1983): 23.

Bennis, Warren. *On Becoming a Leader*. Reading, Mass.: Addison-Wesley, 1989.

Bennis, Warren and Bert Nanus. Leaders: *The Strategies for Taking Charge*. New York: Harper, 1985.

Bernstein, E. and J. Leach. "Plateau." In Albritton and Shaughnessy, *Developing Leadership Skills*. Littleton Colo.: Libraries Unlimited, 1990.

Boyd, D. A. "Leadership, Organizational Dynamics and Rate of Change in Selected Public Libraries in the Northeastern United States." *Dissertation Abstracts International* 41 (1979): 1261A–62A. (University Microfilms No. 8022544).

Dragon, A. C. "Self-Descriptions and Subordinate Descriptions of the Leader Behavior of Library Administrators." *Dissertation Abstracts International* 37 (1976): 7380A–81A. (University Microfilms No. 77-12, 796).

Euster, Joanne R. "Leaders and Managers: Literature Review, Synthesis and a New Conceptual Framework." *Journal of Library Administration* 5, (1984): 45–61.

Gardner, John W. "Leadership Management." In *Leadership Papers*. Washington, D.C.: Independent Sector, 1987.

Gerzog, Alice. "An Investigation into the Relationship between the Structure of Leadership and the Social Structure of the Library Profession." Doctoral dissertation, Rutgers University, 1986.

Gorman, Michael. "A Good Heart and an Organized Mind: Leadership in Technical Services. In *Library Leadership: Visualizing the Future*, edited by Donald E. Riggs. Phoenix, Ariz.: Oryx, 1982.

Kouzes, James, and Barry Posner. *The Leadership Challenge*. San Francisco: Jossey-Bass, 1987.

Lester, June. "Roles of Schools of Library and Information Science." In Woodsworth and Von Wahlde, *Leadership for Research Libraries*. Metuchen, N.J.: Scarecrow, 1988.

Rike, G. E. "Staff Leadership Behavior of Directors of State Library Agencies: A Study of Role Expectations and Perceived Fulfillment." *Dissertation Abstracts International* 37 (1976): 7382A–83A. (University Microfilms No. 77-13343).

Sparks, R. "Library Management: Consideration and Structure." *The Journal of Academic Librarianship* 2 (1976): 66–71.

White, Herbert S. "Oh, Where Have All the Leaders Gone?" *Library Journal* 112 (October 1, 1987): 68.

EPILOGUE

The problem with writing a book on leadership is that the concepts are complex, and there are no simple formulas for success to recommend to aspiring leaders. In fact, what we learn from the experiences of those who have achieved "success" in our field is that although style is important, what is even more important is the ability to be consistent in approach. While creativity and innovation by themselves are much valued, such qualities do not necessarily inspire the trust that brings promotion and recognition.

Our library leaders exhibit the qualities of corporate leadership as described by Bennis and Nanus. They *are* visionary, but they appear to recognize that it is not necessary to be a highly original thinker to be considered a visionary. The skill is to be able to take an idea, give it substance, life, credibility, focus attention on it, gather support for it, and then simply persist until it is accomplished. Our leaders have also learned that focusing on two or three relatively simple goals works better than attempting to follow a complicated agenda that is open to many interpretations.

In addition, the library leaders seem to understand that it doesn't take extraordinary ability and talent to be extraordinarily successful. Just being slightly superior will make a vast difference; the margin of difference that sets apart superior is more often hard work and long hours than creativity and talent.

As in every other field, our leaders very often have to go out on a limb, take risks, commit themselves to an idea or goal that may seem impossible to others. Making the decision to go forward—being the pacesetter—can sometimes be lonely. In such times, leaders must be secure and self-confident and have the inner resources to trust themselves. It is then that the nature of our work, our unshakable belief in its intrinsic worth, sets us apart from the corporate leaders. Personal wealth and corporate profit do not create that "passion for the profession" that I found as a recurring theme among our leaders. Quite simply, the interviewees by and large emerge as dedicated to service rather than profit, and they express a deep conviction that what they do as individuals, and what is accomplished by the profession in general, is significant to society.

While the library leaders recognize that at times the profession may be undervalued (and a few express concern for its future), they are on the whole very optimistic. Since they are relatively content with their own accomplishments, the interviewees do not dwell on questions of status and image. Again, their faith in the societal value of the work comes through.

The leaders enjoy debate; they state their opinions forcefully in professional forums and in the press. In initiating change, however, their strongest tool is their natural ability to actively listen and to trust the group process in making decisions. One of the profession's most respected leaders confided that the low point of her career came when she forgot that the value of power is in sharing it. It is not so much a matter of being humble; it is simple recognition that the higher one's position in the organization, the more dependent the leader is on associates to get the job done.

While the interviews did not elicit a definitive understanding of what distinguishes leaders from non-leaders, they did reinforce Bennis' contention that leadership can be and is exercised at every level of an organization. In most cases, the ability to exercise leadership has more to do with attitude than actual circumstances of the environment. Given a bad supervisor, many employees tend to focus most of their energies on the injustices of the job situation. Leaders, on the other hand, learn what they can from the situation, focus on finding satisfaction in the job itself, work around negative elements, and/or move on to a better environment.

Several of the leaders said that they learned as much or more about leadership behavior (what it isn't) from a "bad boss." It is not easy to step back and look with perspective at a situation in which one is totally immersed, but many of our leaders said they were able to do this at critical points early in their careers.

In listening to the library leaders project excitement and enthusiasm about their work, it is impossible not to speculate about the forces and factors that not only led them to librarianship, but also may have ignited the sparks that led them to uncommon achievement.

Lotsee Patterson attributes her accomplishments to the fact that she had triplets: "For the first time I got a lot of attention . . . the center page of *Parade*. . . . raising five kids was an impossible task and one day I woke up and realized I was not going to go off the deep end . . . I was strong!" Once Patterson recognized that she was strong and self-confident, she had the will and determination to establish a career and to finish her doctoral work. Now she has become involved locally and nationally to improve library services for Native Americans.

For Eric Moon, who was given the *Complete Plays of Bernard Shaw* as a reward for good marks in school (when he expected at least a "gold-plated bicycle"), a giant disappointment turned into power when he saw that he possessed information that others didn't have.

Sixty persons interviewed—and dozens of wonderful incidents that led to careers in librarianship. It has been difficult to avoid the temptation to include many more of these anecdotes than actually necessary to make the points that are pertinent. Herbert White, in speaking of his strengths said, "I have the ability to distinguish between the trivial and the important. . . . many people find it impossible to come to closure. At some point it is necessary to say 'this is not good enough,' make a decision [or turn in the manuscript], and then not look back." My editor has echoed those comments, and so I will conclude with final remarks on the recruitment of the next generation of leaders.

Of all the leaders interviewed, most were encouraged to enter the profession by a strong librarian or faculty member who was not only a role model, but also was quite direct in giving career advice. A recent study (Heim and Moen, 1989) found that of 3,484 library students enrolled in ALA-accredited schools, 35 percent were influenced by librarians to enter the field, far ahead of other influences such as "friends," "faculty," or "family members." While an earlier study (Webb and Pearson, 1986) indicated that personal contact with a librarian is a relatively minor factor in choosing this field, *it was a central influence for many of our leaders.*

Currently, Schools of Library and Information Studies are intent on improving admissions standards, encouraging science and mathematics majors to enter the field, and there is a continuing effort to attract greater numbers of minorities. Practitioners are very important to the success of these efforts. Along with diversity of background, practicing librarians and library educators should also be alert for early signs of a propensity for "attention through vision, meaning through communication, trust through positioning, and positive self-regard."

REFERENCES

Heim, Kathleen M. and William E. Moen. *Occupational Entry: Library and Information Science Students' Attitudes, Demographic and Aspirations Survey.* Chicago: ALA Office for Personnel Resources, 1989.

Webb, T. D. and Richard C. Pearson. "Generalist Training Won't Do." *American Libraries* (November 1986).

APPENDIXES

Persons Interviewed

Millicent (Penny) Abell, University Librarian, Yale University

Toni Bearman, Dean, School of Library and Information Science, University of Pittsburgh

David Bender, Executive Director, Special Libraries Association, Washington, D.C.

Bob Berring, Law Librarian, University of California–Berkeley

John Berry, Editor, *Library Journal*

Lee Brawner, Executive Director, Metropolitan Library System, Oklahoma City

Ching-chih Chen, Associate Dean and Professor, Graduate School of Library and Information Science, Simmons College, Boston

Margaret Chisholm, Director, Graduate School of Library and Information Science, University of Washington

Elizabeth Crabb, Director, Northeast Texas Library System, Garland

Linda Crismond, Executive Director, American Library Association, Chicago

Robert Croneberger, Director, Carnegie Library of Pittsburgh

Jean Curtis, Director, Detroit Public Library

Richard DeGennero, Librarian, Harvard College

Richard Dougherty, Professor, School of Library and Information Studies, University of Michigan

Kenneth E. Dowlin, Director, San Francisco Public Library

Leigh Estabrook, Dean, Graduate School of Library and Information Science, University of Illinois

Thomas J. Galvin, Director, Information Science Doctoral Program, Rockefeller College of Public Affairs and Policy, State University of New York–Albany

Agnes Griffin, Director, Montgomery County Libraries, Maryland

Warren (Jim) Haas, President, Council of Library Resources, Washington, D.C.

Robert Hayes, Dean Emeritus, University of California–Los Angeles

Kathleen M. Heim, Graduate Dean, Louisiana State University, Baton Rouge

David Henington, Director, Houston Public Library

Edward G. Holley, Kenan Professor, University of North Carolina–Chapel Hill

Norman Horrocks, Vice President, Scarecrow Press

E. J. Josey, Professor, School of Library and Information Science, University of Pittsburgh

Margaret Kimmel, Professor, School of Library and Information Science, University of Pittsburgh

Mary Lankford, Coordinator of Library and Media Services, Irving, Texas, Public Schools

Beverly P. Lynch, Dean, Graduate School of Library and Information Science, University of California–Los Angeles

Anne J. Mathews, Director, Office of Library Programs, U.S. Department of Education

Regina Minudri, Director, Berkeley, California, Public Library

Eric Moon, Former President (retired), Scarecrow Press

Patrick O'Brien, Director, Dallas Public Library

Lotsee Patterson, Coordinator, School Libraries, Oklahoma City

Thomas Phelps, Director, Library Programs, National Endowment for the Humanities

Ann Prentice, Vice President for Information, University of South Florida

Jane Robbins, Director, School of Library and Information Studies, University of Wisconsin–Madison

Charles Robinson, Director, Baltimore County Public Library

Carlton Rochell, Dean of Libraries, New York University

Robert Rohlf, Director, Hennepin County Libraries, Minnesota

Joseph Rosenthal, Librarian, University of California–Berkeley

Patricia Schuman, President, Neal-Schuman Publishers, New York

Russell Shank, Assistant Vice Chancellor, Library and Information Services Planning, University of California–Los Angeles

Elliot Shelkrot, Director, Free Library of Philadelphia

Joseph F. Shubert, State Librarian/Assistant Commissioner for Libraries, New York State Education Department, Albany

Elaine Sloan, Dean of Libraries, Columbia University

Elizabeth Snapp, Director, Mary Evelyn Blagg-Huey Library, Texas Woman's University

Elizabeth Stone, Dean Emerita, School of Library and Information Science, Catholic University

Gary Strong, State Librarian, California

Robert Stueart, Dean, Graduate School of Library and Information Science, Simmons College

Peggy Sullivan, Director of Libraries, Northern Illinois University

F. William Summers, Dean, School of Library and Information Studies, Florida State University

Nettie Taylor, Former State Librarian (retired), Maryland Department of Education

Alphonse Trezza, Professor, Florida State University

Robert Warner, Dean, School of Information and Library Studies, University of Michigan

Duane Webster, Executive Director, Association of Research Libraries, Washington, D.C.

Robert Wedgeworth, Dean, School of Library Service, Columbia University

Richard Werking, Director of Libraries, Trinity University, San Antonio

Herbert White, Dean, School of Library and Information Science, Indiana University

Pat Woodrum, Director, Tulsa City-County Library System

Blanche Woolls, Chair, Department of Library Science, School of Library and Information Science, University of Pittsburgh

Conversations

Dorothy J. Anderson, Assistant Dean, Graduate School of Library and Information Science, University of California–Los Angeles

Augusta Baker, Storyteller-in-Residence, College of Library and Information Science, University of South Carolina

Peggy Barber, Associate Executive Director for Communication Services, American Library Association, Chicago

Herbert Bloom, Senior Editor, ALA Books, Chicago

Lillian M. Bradshaw (retired), Director, Dallas Public Library

Richard Budd, Dean, School of Communication, Information, and Library Studies, Rutgers University

Charles A. Bunge, Professor, University of Wisconsin–Madison

Ana and Don Cleveland, School of Library and Information Sciences, University of North Texas

Keith M. Cottam, Director of Libraries, University of Wyoming

Arthur Curley, Director, Boston Public Library

Evelyn Daniel, Professor, University of North Carolina–Chapel Hill

Ann Heidbreder Eastman, Eastman Associates, Blacksburg, Virginia

Sara Fine, Professor, University of Pittsburgh

Hazel Furman (retired), School of Library and Information Studies, Texas Woman's University

Barbara Immroth, Associate Professor, Graduate School of Library and Information Science, University of Texas–Austin

S. Janice Kee (retired), Regional Program Officer, U.S. Department of Education, Fort Worth, Texas

June Lester, Accreditation Officer, American Library Association, Chicago

James M. Matarazzo, Professor, Graduate School of Library and Information Science, Simmons College, Boston

Maxine Merriman, Director of Libraries, General Dynamics, Fort Worth, Texas

Joseph J. Mika, Director, Library Science Program, Wayne State University, Detroit

Bessie Moore, Member, 1991 White House Conference Advisory Board, Little Rock, Arkansas

Margaret Myers, Director, Office for Library Personnel Resources, American Library Association, Chicago

Peggy O'Donnell, Library Consultant, Chicago

Gilda and Felipe de Ortego y Gasca, School of Library and Information Studies, Texas Woman's University, Denton

Roger Parent, Deputy Executive Director, American Library Association, Chicago

Karen Ruddy, Texas Tech University, Lubbock

L. Scott Sheldon, Administrative Librarian for Development, New Mexico State Library, Santa Fe

Patricia M. Smith, Executive Director, Texas Library Association, Austin

Elizabeth Stroup, Director, Seattle Public Library

Herman Totten, Professor, School of Library and Information Science, University of North Texas

Richard L. Waters, Principal Consultant, HBW Associates, Denton, Texas

FURTHER READING

BOOKS

Adams, John. *Transforming Leadership*. Alexandria, Va.: Miles River Press, 1986.

Albritton, Rosie and T. Shaughnessy. *Developing Leadership Skills*. Englewood, Colo.: Libraries Unlimited, 1990.

Bass, Bernard M. *Leadership and Performance beyond Expectation*. New York: Macmillan, 1985.

Bennis, Warren. *On Becoming a Leader*. Reading, Mass.: Addison-Wesley, 1989.

Bennis, Warren and Bert Nanus. *Leaders: The Strategies for Taking Charge*. New York: Harper, 1985.

Blanchard, Kenneth. *Leadership and the One-Minute Manager*. New York: Berkeley, 1986.

Block, Peter. *The Empowered Manager: Positive Political Skills*. San Francisco: Jossey-Bass, 1987.

Boyd, D. A. "Leadership, Organizational Dynamics and Rate of Change in Selected Public Libraries in the Northeastern United States." *Dissertation Abstracts International* 41(1979): 1261A–62A. (University Microfilms No. 8022544).

Burns, James MacGregor. *Leadership*. New York: Harper, 1978.

Cleveland, Harlan. *The Knowledge Executive*. New York: Dutton, 1985.

Dragon, A. C. "Self-Descriptions and Subordinate Descriptions of the Leader Behavior of Library Administrators." *Dissertation Abstracts International* 37 (1976): 7380A–81A. (University Microfilms No. 77-12, 796).

Drucker, Peter F. *Managing the Non-Profit Organization*. New York: Harper/Collins, 1990.

Euster, Joanne R. "Leaders and Managers: Literature Review, Synthesis and a New Conceptual Framework." *Journal of Library Administration* 5 (1984): 45–61.

Fiedler, F. E. *A Theory of Leadership Effectiveness*. New York: McGraw-Hill, 1967.

Gardner, John. *Leadership Papers*. Washington, D.C.: Independent Sector, 1986–88.

Guest, Robert H. *Organizational Change: The Effect of Successful Leadership*. Homewood, Ill.: Dorsey, 1962.

Hagsberg, Janet O. *Real Power: Stages of Personal Power in Organizations*. Minneapolis, Minn.: Winston, 1984.

Hersey, Paul and Kenneth Blanchard. *Management of Organizational Behavior*. New York: Prentice-Hall, 1982.

Hollander, Edwin P. *Leadership Dynamics: A Practical Guide to Effective Relationships*. New York: Macmillan, 1984.

Kanter, Rosabeth Moss. *When Giants Learn to Dance*. New York: Simon & Schuster, 1989.

Kotter, John P. *The Leadership Factor*. New York: Free Press, 1988.

Kouzes, James and Barry Posner. *The Leadership Challenge*. San Francisco: Jossey-Bass, 1987.

———. *On Leadership*. New York: Free Press, 1990.

Riggs, Donald E. and Gordon Sabine. *Libraries in the Nineties: What the Leaders Expect*. Phoenix, Ariz.: Oryx, 1988.

Rike, G. E. "Staff Leadership Behavior of Directors of State Library Agencies: A Study of Role Expectations and Perceived Fulfillment." *Dissertation Abstracts International* 37 (1976): 7382A–83A. (University Microfilms No. 77-13343).

Rosenbach, William and Robert Taylor. *Contemporary Issues in Leadership*. Boulder, Colo.: Westview, 1984.

Sparks, Rita. "Library Management: Consideration and Structure." *Journal of Academic Librarianship* 2 (1976):66–71.

Timpe, Dale A. *Leadership*. New York: Facts on File, c1987.

Woodsworth, Anne and B. Von Wahlde. *Leadership for Research Libraries*. A Festschrift for Robert M. Hayes. Metuchen, N.J.: Scarecrow, 1988.

Yukl, Gary. *Leadership in Organizations*. New York: Prentice-Hall, 1981.

ARTICLES

Cheney, Lynne. "My Turn." *Newsweek*, August 11, 1990.

Cleese, John. "No More Mistakes and You're Through." *Forbes*, May 16, 1988, pp. 126+.

Duszak, Thomas. "Leaders in Libraries: A Pennsylvania Perspective." Unpublished paper presented at the Pennsylvania Library Association meeting, 1986.

McCall, Morgan W., and Michael Lombardo."What Makes a Top Executive?" *Psychology Today*, February 1983.

Mitchell, Eugene S. "A Review of Leadership Research." Unpublished manuscript, Library Administration and Management Association, July 1988.

White, Herbert S. "Oh, Where Have All the Leaders Gone?" *Library Journal*, October 1, 1987, pp. 68–69.

Zalenznik, Abraham. "Managers and Leaders: Are They Different?" *Harvard Business Review* 55 (May–June 1977): 162–79.

Brooke E. Sheldon is Dean of the Graduate School of Library and Information Science at the University of Texas at Austin. She has lectured and conducted workshops and seminars throughout the United States and abroad on various aspects of management, including planning and evaluation of library projects, grant proposal writing, communications skills, and leadership. Her publications include *Planning and Evaluating Library Training Programs* for the U.S. Office of Education, a number of evaluative studies and articles relating to management, continuing education, and issues and trends in librarianship. In 1983–84, Sheldon served as President of the American Library Association. She holds a doctorate in library and information science from the University of Pittsburgh and an M.L.S. from Simmons College.